Value Driven Project Management Using Prince2

ISBN-13: 978-1477454565

ISBN-10: 147745456X

Copyright © 2012 Pankaj Sharma, PMP, Prince Practitioner

ABOUT THE AUTHOR

Pankaj Sharma is a project management consultant and trainer with over 15 years of practical 'hands-on' project and program management experience in managing and directing mid and large sized IT program/projects involving distributed teams in Manufacturing, HR and healthcare verticals across US, Europe and UK geography.

Pankaj Holds Master degree in computer engineering from Birla Institute of technology and Science, Pilani (India) and is a certified PMP, ITIL v3 and a Prince2 practitioner. Enriched with long industry experience, coupled with excellent professional track record, Pankaj is extremely passionate about sharing his professional knowledge and experience. He has coached employees from the companies IBM, Accenture, Deloitte, Birlasoft, HCL, TCS and Indian defense forces (Army, Navy and Indian Air force). Presently he is Chief Technology Officer for Connoisseur Consulting Solutions Pvt Ltd and in the current role he is responsible for IT and business Strategy management.

Contents at a Glance

Chapter 1 – Introduction to Prince2 4
    What is PRINCE2? 4
    History of PRINCE 2 4
    Why Prince2 5
    PRINCE2 Foundation & Practitioner Exams 5

Chapter 2 - Project Management Basics 8
    What is a Project? 8
    Characteristics of Projects 9
    Projects versus Operations 10
    Why Projects Fail? 11
    SMART Objectives 12
    What is Project Management? 12
    What is the role of Project Manager? 12
    What are Project Stakeholders? 14
    Prince2 Project Organization Structure 15

Chapter 3 – Prince2 Integrated Elements 16

Chapter 4 - Processes 21
    Starting Up a Project 21
    Initiating a Project 23
    Controlling a Stage 27
    Managing Product Delivery Process 28
    Managing a Stage Boundary 29
    Closing a Project 30

Chapter 5 – Themes 33
    Business Case 33
    Organization 42
    Quality 46
    Plan 51
    Risk 62
    Change Theme 69
    Progress Theme 73

Chapter 6 – Management Products 78

Sample Paper -1 83
Sample Paper - 2 118
Sample Paper - 3 154
Sample Paper - 4 184
Practitioner Exam Tips 220

Chapter1 – Introduction to Prince2

What is PRINCE2?

PRINCE2 is an acronym for "Projects IN Controlled Environments", 2nd version. It's a structured project management methodology for managing the projects effectively.

PRINCE2 can be tailored and applied to any project regardless of project scale, type, organization, geography or culture.

History of PRINCE 2

PRINCE2 methodology was first established in 1989 by the British Government's CCTA (the Central Computer and Telecommunications Agency), which is now the office of Government Commerce (OGC).

The method was originally based on PROMPT, a project management method created Simpact Systems Ltd in 1975. PROMPT was adopted by CCTA in 1979 as standard to be used for all government information system projects. When PRINCE2 was launched in 1989, it effectively superseded PROMPT within government projects.

OGC continued to develop the method launching PRINCE2 in 1996 in response to user requirements for improved guidance on project management on all projects, not just information systems.

Why Prince2

- Widely recognized Project Management Certification
- Demonstrates **Proof** of Professional Achievement
- The structured approach to plan, execute and monitor helps in managing the project effectively
- Increases your **Marketability and Employment Prospects** as many companies across the globe want their staff to be Prince2 certified.
- Displays your willingness to pursue **Growth**
- **Increases** Customer Confidence
- Valued Globally across **Industry Verticals & Companies**

PRINCE2 Foundation & Practitioner Exams

Following two examinations applicable to PRINCE2:

- Foundation examination
- Practitioner examination

Foundation Examination Details

The Foundation is the first of the two PRINCE2 Examinations you are required to pass to become a PRINCE2Practitioner. This is a basic level exam that aims to measure whether a candidate would be able to act as an informed member of a project management team using the PRINCE2 method within a project environment supporting PRINCE2. The candidate should have good understanding of

- Four Integrated Elements of Prince2 - Principles ,Processes, Themes and the Project Environment
- Prince2 Project organization structure, key roles and the responsibilities associated with the roles
- Purpose and Contents of the major management products

Foundation Exam Format

Multiple-choice

One hour duration

75 questions

35 correct answers are required to pass

Closed-book

Practitioner Examination Details

The Practitioner is the second of the two PRINCE2 Examinations you are required to pass to become a PRINCE2 Practitioner.

This level aims to assess whether a candidate would be able to apply PRINCE2 to the real time project within an environment supporting PRINCE2. To demonstrate this candidate needs to exhibit the competence required for the Foundation qualification, and show that they can apply and tune PRINCE2 to address the needs and problems of a specific project.

Precisely the candidates must be able to:

Produce detailed explanations of all processes, components and techniques, and worked examples of all PRINCE2 products as they might be applied to address the particular circumstances of a given project scenario.

Show they understand the relationships between Principle, Themes, Processes and the PRINCE2 products and can apply this understanding.

Demonstrate their ability to tailor PRINCE2 to different project environments.

Practitioner Exam Format

The Practitioner exam presents the following main characteristics:

9 questions, with a scenario background and appendices

Each of the 9 questions is worth 12 marks

An overall score of 59 out of possible 108 is required to pass (55%)

2.5 hours duration

Open book examination (only the PRINCE2 Manual is allowed)

For Practitioners & Registered Practitioners

All PRINCE2 Practitioners should be re-registered within 5 years of their original certification. This Re-Registration comprises a 1-hour examination set at the same standard as the Practitioner examination.

Chapter 2 - Project Management Basics

What is a Project?

PRINCE2 Definition

"A temporary organization that is created for the purpose of delivering one or more business Products according to an agreed Business Case"

Some of the other Project Management frameworks define project as:

"A temporary Endeavour undertaken to create a unique product, service or result"

Some examples of the project are:

- Filming a Motion Picture
- Construction of a building – Office, Hospital or a shopping mall
- Moving the office from one building to another
- Hosting an event
- Creating a new process
- Creating a Product
- Developing a software
- Implementing a software product
- Major Enhancement to a Software

Characteristics of Projects

- They bring about **Change**. All the projects brings change, the change can be in the form of process, products, tools and techniques, organization structure or at the least expectations.

- They are **temporary** (They have a defined **Start** and a defined **End).**

- They are usually **Cross-functional.** Projects involve a team of people with different skills working together. Examples – Engineers, Testers, Business Analyst and so on.

- Every Project is **Unique.** Though there may be common elements in the project but the two projects will differ in terms of the team, location and environment. Example constructing a shopping mall providing similar offerings in two different locations.

- There is a degree of Uncertainty associated with all the projects

- Projects are progressively elaborated. A project starts with a vision or goal. The goal is converted into a high level plan and as you proceed forward the requirements unfold and you get more clarity on the requirements and this helps you to plan the immediate future at a detailed level.

The diagram below depicts High level view of a project life cycle (Single Phase)

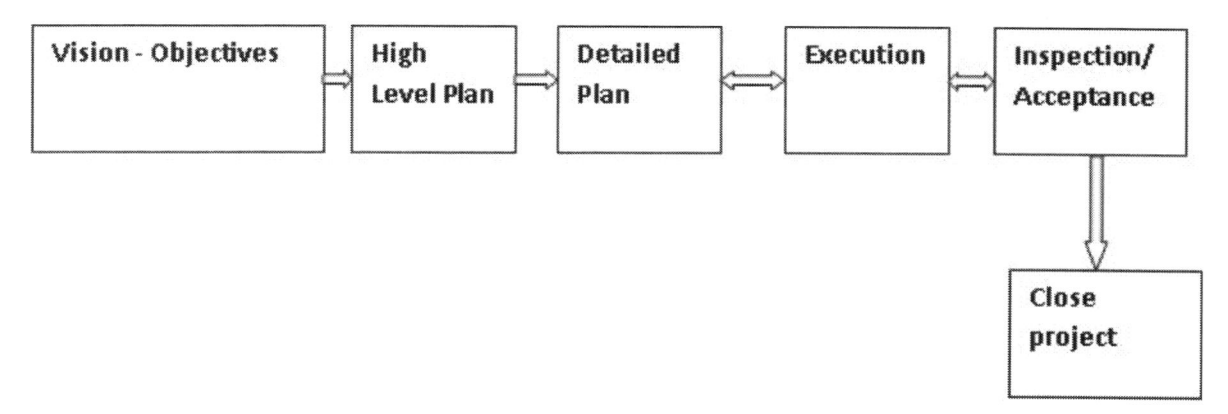

Vision - Objectives → High Level Plan → Detailed Plan ⇄ Execution ⇄ Inspection/ Acceptance → Close project

Projects versus Operations

Operations are ongoing and produce repetitive products, services, or results. Operations work is ongoing that sustains the organization over time.

- Operations and projects differ in the way that operations are **ongoing** but projects are **temporary**.
- Operations are **repetitive** in nature while projects create a **unique** product or service.
- Operations objective is to **sustain** business while project **closes** after the objectives are achieved.

Examples of Operations

- Assembly line production
- Call center operations – Help desk, customer service, and so on

PROJECTS	OPERATIONS
Temporary	Ongoing
Unique	Repetitive
Closes after attaining the objectives	Objective is to sustain business
Examples are : Launching the new car model	Examples are : Assembly line production, Monthly Payroll

Most of the times projects fail due to lousy project management. Some of the major reasons are:

- Lack of clearly defined purpose
- Poor requirements and scope management
- Poor estimation of duration and cost
- Project Managers lacking in General Management skills
- Cultural and ethical misalignment
- Poor communication or lack of coordination of resources and activities
- Inadequate planning of scope, schedule, resources, cost, risk and quality
- Lack of Monitoring and Control resulting into poor quality of deliverables

SMART Objectives

Setting up clear objectives and constantly reminding the team about those objectives is critically important for the success of a project

. A simple acronym used to set objectives is called SMART objectives. SMART stands for Specific, Measurable, Achievable and time bound.

An example of a SMART objective is:

Implement an ERP to reduce the overall the inventory cost by 1 million USD in a time frame of 14 months.

What is Project Management?

Project Management is the application of knowledge, skills, tools and techniques to project activities to meet the project requirements.

The project team carries out the work needed to complete the project, while the project manager schedules, monitors, and controls the various project tasks. The project manager requires **knowledge**, **performance,** and **personal** skills to perform better at their jobs.

The typical work of a project manager involves:

- **Requirements gathering**
- **Managing stakeholder expectations**
- **Managing key projects Aspect** including scope, quality, schedule, resources, Benefits, and risk.

What is the role of Project Manager?

The role of a Project Manager is to achieve project objectives. It is different from the role of a functional or operations manager. The functional manager provides management oversight for an administrative area. The operations managers are accountable for a facet of the core business.

Effective project management requires a Project Manager to have

- Understanding and skills to apply Project Management tools and techniques
- Good General Management Skills

General Management Skills are most important skills required by a project manager and this include.

- Communication Skills

- Organization and Planning Skills
- Budgeting Skills
- Conflict Management Skills
- Negotiation and Influencing Skills
- Leadership Skills
- Team – Building and Motivating Skills

A project manager spends about 90% of time communicating out which more than 50% of his time is spent in communicating with the team

What are Project Stakeholders?

Project stakeholders are individuals and organizations involved in the project that will be directly or indirectly impacted by the outcome of the project. The stakeholders may have positive or negative influence on the outcome of the project.

The stakeholders must be identified early in the project. This is often a difficult task. The project manager needs to manage the expectations of the key stakeholders to successfully complete the project.

Key stakeholders include:

- Project Manager
- Customer / User
- Performing organization/Supplier
- Project team members
- Project management team
- Sponsor
- Influencers

Stakeholders can be internal or external to the project team.

Prince2 Project Organization Structure

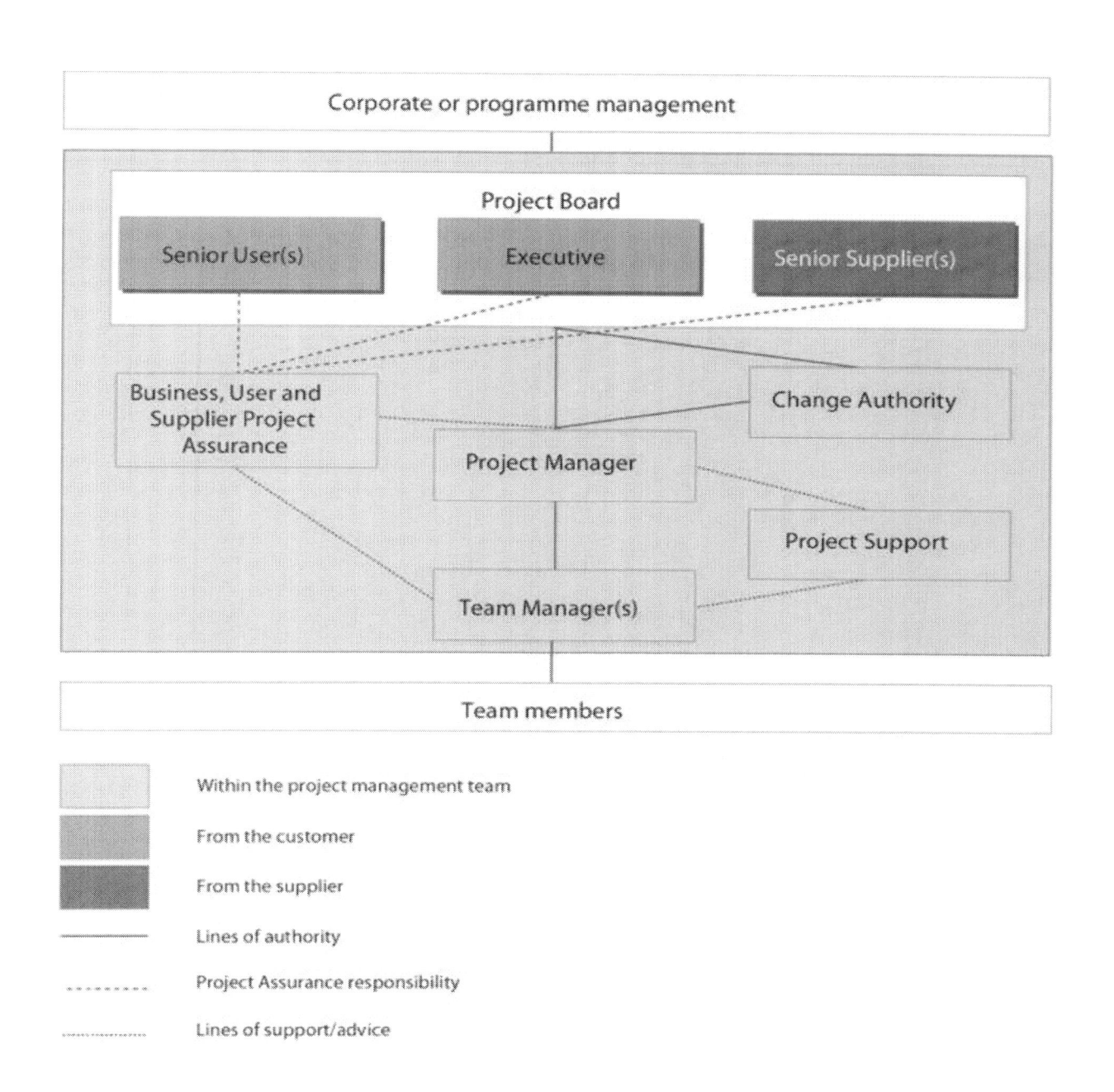

Project Board

- Senior User(s)
- Executive
- Senior Supplier(s)

Corporate or programme management

Business, User and Supplier Project Assurance

Change Authority

Project Manager

Project Support

Team Manager(s)

Team members

Legend:
- Within the project management team
- From the customer
- From the supplier
- ——— Lines of authority
- ---------- Project Assurance responsibility
- ············ Lines of support/advice

Chapter 3 – Prince2 Integrated Elements

The PRINCE2 methodology is based on four integrated elements and these elements are **Principles, Themes, Processes and the Project Environment** as depicted in the figure below.

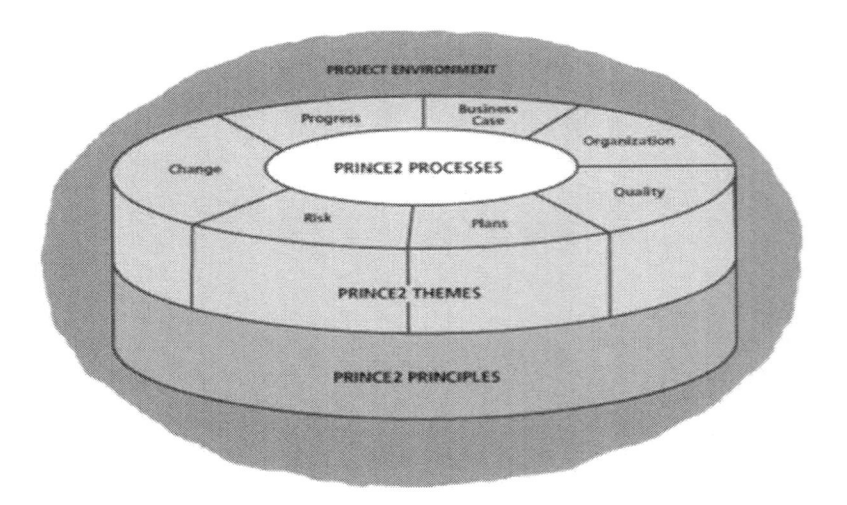

PRINCIPLES

These are the best practices and guidelines which are mandatory for projects that are managed using PRINCE2 methodology. There are seven principles and unless all of them are applied, it is not a PRINCE 2 project. These seven Principles are:

- **Continual Business Justification:** A prince2 project must have justifiable reason to start and continue in any time during project life cycle.

- **Learn from Experience:** At the start of Prince2 project, it is important to review lesson learned from previous or similar projects in order for the project team to see if lessons learned could be applied. It helps in early identification of risks and prevents the reoccurrence of the same problem. As work progresses on the project, lessons are collected, recorded in relevant logs and acted upon throughout the project's lifecycle.

- **Define Roles and Responsibilities:** It is important for everyone in the project team to know what is expected from them in terms of responsibilities, their level of authority for taking decisions and who they report to. In prince2 the roles and responsibilities can be tailored as per the complexity of the project. The project management team is defined much earlier than the start of the project, however it is refined if required throughout the project management life cycle.

- **Manage by Stages:** A project must be broken down into a number of management stages, and after each stage there should be a stage end review to evaluate actual achievement vis-à-vis the planned targets and the viability of the business case. The stage end assessment gives the true picture of the progress and reduces the project risk by timely responding to the uncertainties and quick corrective actions for the issues. Before proceeding to the next stage, the updated Business Case is reviewed to determine whether the project continues to have business justification. If it does, then the project can move into the next stage.

    Every project must have two stages, a stage called the initiation stage which is where a detailed Business Case, Project Plan, and strategies for managing risks, issues, changes, quality, products and communications are developed. Subsequently, there are one or more "delivery" stages which are management stages the where specialist products are developed.

- **Manage by Exception:** Senior manager's time is important and to use it efficiently they should be only involved in a decision making process when it is absolutely necessary. The day to day management is the responsibility of the project manager. The senior management therefore delegates day to day management for a stage to the project manager within agreed "tolerances" for the objectives of scope, time, cost, risk, quality, and Benefits. However, if the project manager forecasts that the Actuals might exceed the allowable tolerances then this is known as an "exception" in PRINCE2 and this must be escalated to the senior management for a decision.

- **Focus on Products:** The focus should be on project outputs/deliverables not on activities. The definition of what the project must deliver or project requirements should be done before the project begins during the high level planning phase. In PRINCE2 this is termed as Project Product Description and is written in consultation with the users. By developing and agreeing on the project requirements early helps in common understanding of the project requirement and the quality expectations from them. It also helps in developing initial cost and time estimates. During the detailed planning stage more detailed descriptions along with their quality expectations for the major products of the project are developed. Based on the detailed product descriptions the products are produced in the subsequent delivery stages.

- **Tailor to suit the project environment:** No two projects are the same. The level of control required for a large complex project is much greater than that required for a project a small project. As the risks associated with complex projects are high the numbers of stages required are likely to be greater than a low risk project. If a similar set of processes are applied to every project without taking into account the complexity there won't be any benefit, in fact sometimes the processes might become overhead instead of an aid. So practitioners must tailor PRINCE2 to suit the needs of the project environment.

THEMES

Seven themes describe the various project management disciplines or areas that must be addresses continually and throughout the project lifecycle. These seven themes are described below in brief.

- **Business Case:** The Business Case justifies initial and continuing investment in a project. Outline Business Case is developed during the high level planning stage; it is detailed during the detailed planning stage and is continuously evaluated and if required updated at the end of subsequent delivery stages during the project life cycle. It helps project management team to assess if a project is desirable, viable and achievable at any point in time. After project closure, the Business Case is confirmed based upon the operational benefits that accrue from using the project's product.

- **Organization:** The Organization theme defines and establishes project roles and responsibilities for a PRINCE2 project. It clearly addresses the three project interests: business, user and supplier. The levels of management for the project are defined across four levels: corporate or program management (External to the project team) who is responsible for commissioning the project, the project board providing overall direction and management (governance), the project manager managing the project's day-to-day activities and team managers delivering the project's technical or specialist products.

- **Quality:** In PRINCE2, quality focuses on ensuring that the project's products are fit for purpose. The approach, defined in the project's Quality Management Strategy, requires that there be an explicit understanding of project scope and the quality criteria against which the products will be assessed. In other words, the focus of quality is on each product's ability to meet its requirements. PRINCE2 contains product-focused elements of quality planning, quality control and quality assurance. Two types of quality methods are advocated: 'in process' methods that build quality into products as they are developed and 'appraisal' methods used to assess if finished products are complete and fit for purpose.

- **Plans:** Plans define how, where and by whom the project's products will be delivered. Plans are used in PRINCE2 to provide facilitate effective communication and control. They are aligned with the Business Case and require both approval and commitment from all levels of the project management team. There are three levels of plan in a project: Project Plan, Stage Plan and Team Plans. In addition, Exception Plans may replace one of the plans when there is a need to re-plan due to a tolerance violation. PRINCE2 requires that product-based planning techniques be used – identifying the products first, and then the dependencies, activities and resources needed to successfully deliver those products.

- **Risks:** are uncertain events that can have positive or negative impact on project objectives. Risk management targets the proactive identification, assessment and control of project risks in order to improve the chances of success. The strategy for approaching risk management in a project is defined in the Risk Management Strategy, created during the initiation stage of the project. The five steps for managing risks are:

    o Identify the cause, event and effects of each risk
    o Assess their probability and impact
    o Plan the specific management responses
    o Implement the risk responses as required
    o Communicate risk information internal and external to the project.

- **Change:** The Change theme in PRINCE2 encompasses configuration management, issue management and change control. Project controls are established and maintained throughout the project to address these three areas. Configuration management creates, maintains and controls the configuration throughout the life of a product. Issues are any event that has happened on a PRINCE2 project that was not planned and requires management action. They can be raised by anyone at any time during the project, and are categorized as a request for change, an off-specification or a problem/concern.

- **Progress:** Progress refers to the mechanisms used to monitor and compare the actual project progress and performance against the planned values. These mechanisms also allow the project manager to proactively forecast future performance based upon current trends relative to project objectives and make decisions to address potential variations. Progress measures the achievement of the objectives of a plan, and can be reviewed at project, stage and work package levels in a project. PRINCE2 uses the concept of tolerance (relative to time, cost, scope, risk, quality, benefits) to implement the principle of 'management by exception'. Each level of plan has tolerances associated with it, allowing the responsible party to make decisions and just get on with things unless a tolerance violation occurs or is predicted to occur in the future. It is important to note that PRINCE2 does not address detailed planning and control techniques that organizations may select to support the PRINCE2 themes, such as critical path or earned value analysis. These techniques are well documented elsewhere and may be incorporated into PRINCE2 at the organization's discretion. Leadership, motivational and other interpersonal skills are also not codified in the method, but are recognized as essential to successful project management.

PROCESSES

These are the collection of activities and describe a step-wise progression through the project lifecycle, from getting started to project closure. A process includes all the roles, responsibilities, tools, metrics and management controls required to reliably deliver the outputs.

The seven processes listed below describe the project lifecycle from getting started to project closure.

1. Starting Up a Project
2. Initiating a Project
3. Controlling a Stage
4. Managing Product Delivery
5. Managing a Stage Boundary
6. Directing a Project
7. Closing a Project

Chapter 4 - Processes

As shared in the process overview in the previous chapter processes are the collections of activities and describe a step-wise progression through the project lifecycle, from getting started to project closure. A process includes all the roles, responsibilities, tools, metrics and management controls required to reliably deliver the outputs.

The seven processes in Prince2 are described in details below:

Starting Up a Project

The 'starting up a project' process ensures that sufficient planning is in place before initiating a project. The process is triggered after the mandate is received from the corporate program management. The primary output of this process is project brief.

The **six activities** performed within 'starting up a project' process are detailed below along with their outputs.

1. **Appoint the Executive and Project Manager**

Programme or Corporate Management provide the Project mandate and create the Executive role description. An executive is appointed who in turn creates the Project Manager Role description and appoints the PM. The PM creates a Daily Log.

2. **Capture Previous Lessons**

Lessons from previous related projects are reviewed and if necessary inserted into the Lessons Log created by the project manager.

3. **Design and Appoint Project Management Team**

The Project manager creates Project Management team structure and the team's role descriptions which are approved by the Executive. The Executive appoints the project management team.

4. **Prepare the Outline Business Case**

The Outline Business Case is a high level view which will be used as a foundation for the detailed business case in the 'initiating a project' process. The Executive prepares the Outline Business Case which should be approved by the corporate Program Management.

5. Create Project Product Description

The Project Manager creates the Project Product Description that describes the high level deliverable for the project and some really useful information, such as the customer's quality expectations and acceptance criteria. All of which helps both with planning and getting sign-off at the end.

6. Select the project approach and assemble the Project Brief

The 'project approach' is the outcome of a series of decisions about how the project and its products will be delivered. For example, off-the-shelf or custom designed products? In-house or 3rd Party development? Modification of existing products, or brand-new ones ? The approach to the project will also be partly defined by pre-existing standards or methods of working of the internal or external suppliers.

A Project Brief is then assembled which: defines the project; incorporates the Outline Business Case, Project Product Description, the project approach and the project management team structure and role descriptions; and prepares any additional role descriptions needed. The Daily Log is updated with additional risks or issues.

The project manager is responsible for creating the project approach and additional role descriptions, assembling the Project Brief and updating the Daily Log.

7. Plan the initiation stage

The Project Manager uses the Project Brief, Daily Log and Lessons Log as inputs in the preparation of a stage plan for the initiation stage. The Project Manager also updates the Daily Log with any new issues or risks.

8. Triggers the directing the project process with request to initiate the project

Sends the Project Brief to the project Board for Approval .Project Board reviews the project Brief and evaluates whether it's worth to go ahead with the detailed planning stage or not. If the Project Board approves then only the initiation stage begins.

Initiating a Project

The objective of Initiating a Project Process is to establish solid foundations for the project before there is a commitment to significant spending. The key objective of this process is to ensure that there is a common understanding of Benefits and Risks, Scope, Timescales and costs, Human resources involved Customer quality expectations and the acceptance criteria.

The key activities performed in this process are:

1. **Prepare Risk Management Strategy**

It outlines the way in which risk will be identified, assessed, responded and communicated during the project management lifecycle. It also describes who should be responsible for carrying out the various risk management roles.

2. **Prepare Configuration Management Strategy**

Configuration management is important for maintaining control over Project's management and specialist products. It defines the processes and procedures related Planning, identification, control, status accounting, verification and audit of the configurable items as explained below:

- How the products and the various versions and variants of these will be identified
- How and where the project's products will be stored and the tools used. This can be a server, or specialized tools such as VSS, CVS or SharePoint.
- What storage and retrieval security will be put in place
- When the configuration management activities should occur and how the performance of the configuration management procedure should be reported
- How changes to products will be controlled
- Roles and responsibilities related to configuration Management

3. **Prepare the Quality Management Strategy (QMS)**

   Quality Management Strategy defines the quality techniques and standards to be applied, and the people responsible for achieving the required quality levels, during the project life cycle. The quality planning starts very early in the project life cycle right at the start up stage when the project product description, customer's quality expectations and the project acceptance criteria is created. During the detailed planning phase the description of the products of the project and the acceptance criteria is created. While designing the quality strategy some of the key things that need to be taken into consideration are:

   - Adherence to the corporate level standards for quality.
   - The projects are executed in buyer and supplier environment so both customer and supply-side must be involved in determining the quality standards, and how they should be applied to this project.
   - Lessons learned from previous similar projects should be captured and used to help define the Quality Management Strategy.
   - The Quality Management Strategy should include the following key information:
     - Quality management procedure to be followed
     - Records that will be checked including tools and techniques to be used
     - How reporting on the quality management procedure performance will occur
     - The roles and responsibilities for quality management activities, including linkages if required, to corporate or programme quality assurance functions.
   - The Quality Management Strategy needs to be reviewed by Project Assurance.

4. Prepare the Communication Management Strategy

A Communication Management Strategy describes the means and frequency of communication to stakeholders that are internal as well as external to the project. In simple words the communication management strategy describes what information should be send to whom, through what means and what frequency and who will be the sender and receiver of the communication. It includes

- Identifying all the internal and external stakeholders. Stakeholder analysis to understand the interest and influence of the stakeholders on the project and consolidating a stakeholder management strategy.
- Communication Procedure: A description of (or reference to) any communication methods to be used, with any variance from the corporate or program management standards highlighted, together with a justification for the variance.
- Tools and Techniques: Refers to communication technology that can be used. It can be pull based technology such as portal or a push based technology such as email.
- Records: Defines what communication records will be required and where they will be stored (for example, logging of external correspondence)
- Reporting: Describes any reports on the communication process that are to be produced, including their purpose, timing and recipients (for example, performance indicators)
- Timing of Communication Activities: States when formal communication activities are to be undertaken (for example, at the end of a stage) including performance audits for the communication methods
- Roles and Responsibilities: Describes who will be responsible for what aspects of the communication process, including any corporate or program management roles involved with communication
- Information Needs for each interested party: Defines the information required to be provided from the project as well as any information required to be provided to the project, including information providers/recipients, frequency of communication, means of communication and format of the communication

- o When the Communication Management Strategy is complete, check it against the quality criteria to ensure it is complete and correct. The criteria include:
  - All stakeholders have been identified and consulted for their communication requirements
  - There is agreement from all stakeholders about the content, frequency and method of communication
  - A common standard for communication has been considered
  - The time, effort and resources required to carry out the identified communications have been allowed for in Stage Plans
  - The formality and frequency of communication is reasonable for the projects importance and complexity

5. Set up the Project Controls

Project controls are set up to ensure that there is a right mechanism to review the project from Board's and Project Manager's perspective. This includes

- Setting frequency and formats of Checkpoint and Highlight reports
- End stage assessments for number of stages
- Procedure for Escalation of exceptions and tolerances at various levels
- Review of Lessons Log, Risk and Issues Registers
- Review QMS, Risk Management Strategy and Config Management Strategy to establish which controls are needed
- Confirm and document the Management Stage Boundaries
- Establish decision-making procedures and levels of authority
- Integrate decision-making levels with the Project Management Team structure and roles and responsibilities
- Summarize project controls in the PID
- Consult Project Assurance to ensure proposed controls comply with standards
- Update Risk register, Issue register and Daily Log as appropriate
- Seek Project Board approval for the project controls

6. Create the Project Plan

The Project manager should involve users and suppliers in creating the plan. Recommended actions are:

- Decide on format and presentation of the plan
- Create product breakdown structure, flow diagram and descriptions for all major products
- Create a Product Flow diagram
- Sequence activities using project network diagram
- Estimate Resources, Duration and Cost

- Baseline Plan

7. Refine the Business Case

- Review Project Brief, Lessons Log and previous similar projects
- Create detailed Business case and the Benefit Review Plan
- Consult Project Assurance to ensure the Business case and Benefits Review Plan comply with standards

8. Assemble the Project Initiation Document (PID)

- Assemble the PID, review it and consult Project Assurance to ensure that the PID meets the requirements
- Prepare the plan for the next stage
- Seek Approval for the PID from the project board.

Controlling a Stage

The purpose of the Controlling a Stage process is to assign work to be done to the specialist teams, monitor such work, manage risks and issues, report progress of the stage to the Project Board, and if required take corrective actions to ensure that the stage remains within tolerance in terms of the six aspects (Scope, Time, Cost, Risk, Quality and Benefits). Some of the key activities in controlling a Stage process are:

- Authorize a Work Package as a result of approval of a stage or an exception plan by the board. Obtain the product descriptions of the entire product to be included in the Work Package and define the techniques, processes and procedures to be used.
- Review a Work Package Status through Checkpoint Reports and receive completed Work Packages
- Review the team plan with team manager to forecast whether the work will be completed on time and budget.
- Review the Project Initiation document for the project controls such as reporting method required, Quality Management Strategy and the Quality standards required, Configuration management strategy for how the products are to be hand over
- Reviewing the product quality and triggering the new Work Package or update the existing ones.
- Review entries in the Quality Register related to products in the work package to understand the current status of quality management activities and ensure that each product in the Work Package has gained its requisite approval.
- Confirm that the configuration item record for each approved product is updated
- Update the stage plan to show the Work Package as completed
- Review the Stage Plan (current stage) for products to be produced, cost, effort and tolerances available
- Review the stage status, report highlights and take corrective actions if required.

- Watching for, assessing and dealing with issues and risks. This includes maintaining Issue and Risk registers. Escalate Issues and Risks

Optionally, the controlling a stage process may be used during the initiation stage, particularly if this stage is lengthy or risky.

Managing Product Delivery Process

Specialist products are delivered, tested and accepted in this process.

The purpose of the Managing Product Delivery process is to control the link between the Project Manager and the Team Manager(s), by placing formal requirements on accepting, executing and delivering project work.

The role of the Team Manager(s) is to coordinate an area of work that will deliver one or more of the project's products. They can be internal or external to the customer's organization. The key activities in Managing Product Delivery process are:

- Work on products allocated to the team is authorized and agreed
- Team Managers, team members and suppliers are clear as to what is to be produced and what is the expected effort, cost or timescales
- The planned products are delivered to expectations and within tolerance
- Accurate progress information in the form of checkpoint reports is provided to the Project Manager at an agreed frequency to ensure that expectations are managed.
- Products that are created or updated during this process are:
  - Team plans with actual dates.
  - Risk register with any identified work package level risks.
  - Quality register with all quality work that is being undertaken.
  - Configuration Item Records with the latest status of products produced.
  - Project Issues with status information and impact analysis for current or new issues identified.
  - Checkpoint Reports providing regular progress information to the Project Manager.

Managing a Stage Boundary

The purpose of this process is to aid Project Board in making an informed choice about whether to continue with the project or not on the basis of information provided by the project manager on performance of the current stage. The project should only continue if there is a business justification for the project, we should not proceed with a project and waste effort and money it the products created doesn't deliver the benefits expected from them. This process is performed near the end of every stage except the final stage where closing the project process is performed. The key activities performed in this stage are:

- Ensure and communicate to the Project Board that all products in the Stage Plan for the current stage have been completed and approved
- Review and, if necessary, update the Project Initiation Documentation (in particular the Business Case, Project Plan, project approach, strategies, project management team structure and role descriptions)
- Provide the information needed for the Project Board to assess the continuing viability of the project and the aggregated risk exposure such as

    o An End Stage Report produced by the Project Manager and given to the Project Board, outlining information on the current stage achievements.
    o Current Stage Plan Actuals showing the performance against the original Stage Plan
    o An updated Risk register, together with the Updated Business Case and Project Plan, which is used by the Project Board to review that the Project has continuing ongoing viability.
    o An updated Configurable item record and Product Status Account
- Any changes to the Project Management Team with updated Job Descriptions.

Closing a Project

The purpose of this process is to execute a controlled close to the project.
The process covers the Project Manager's work to wrap up the project either at its end or at premature close.
Most of the work is to prepare input to the Project Board to obtain its confirmation that the project may close.

The objectives of this process are therefore to:

- Check the extent to which the objectives or aims set out in the Project Initiation Document (PID) have been met
- Confirm the extent of the fulfillment of the Project Initiation Document (PID) and the Customer's satisfaction with the deliverables
- Obtain formal acceptance of the deliverables
- Ensure to what extent all expected products have been handed over and accepted by the Customer
- Confirm that maintenance and operation arrangements are in place (where appropriate)
- Make any recommendations for follow-on actions
- Capture lessons resulting from the project and complete the Lessons Learned Report
- Prepare an End Project Report
- Notify the host organization of the intention to disband the project organization and resources.

Directing a Project

The Project Board is accountable for this process and the purpose of this process is to support Project Manager by providing direction on adhoc basis and authorization at critical points such as Start up, Initiating, Delivery stages of the project and in case of exception at a stage level. The project board is accountable for the project's success and has to ensure that key decisions are made while exercising overall control. It delegates day-to-day management of the project to the project manager, and release the project to the project manager one stage at a time. This process is triggered by the project manager's request to initiate the project and the key activities performed by the Project Board in this process are:

- Authorize Initiation
- Authorize the Project
- Authorize the Stage Plan
- Ensure that there is authority to deliver the project products
- Give adhoc direction to the project team and ensure that the project remains viable and management direction and control are in place throughout the projects life.
- Provide regular updates to the corporate or programme management on the progress of the project
- Authorize project closure
- A benefit review plan for realizing the post project benefits is created, managed and reviewed.
- Exception Assessment and Authorize the Exception plan. The project board uses the technique management by exception. It monitors via reports and provides control via a number of the decision points. For management by exception to work, the project board must set tolerance, and if at any point this is forecasted to be exceeded, the project manager will inform the project board via an Exception Report to bring the situation to the project board's attention.
- Although it is the executive of the project board who has the veto on any decisions and direction given, the project board should provide a unified direction and guidance to the project manager and other key stakeholders. The project board is responsible for assuring that there is continued business justification, and this is why the project Board Executive owns the project Business Case.

Chapter 5 – Themes

Business Case

The Business Case describes the business justification of the project, it explains whether the investment in the project is worthwhile or not. An outline Business Case is created at the start up stage and is used to determine if it is worth investing in the initiation stage. The detailed Business Case forms part of the Project Initiation Documentation and is used by the project board to determine if it is worthwhile to go ahead with the project.

The Business case of a project can be based on financial benefits (Based on ROI, NPV and so on) as well as other reasons such as ;

Mandatory Project: The projects that are initiated to fulfill some government mandate, rules or regulation.

Not – for – profit project: The NGO projects such as improving the literacy rate of a particular state by 25% or to reduce poverty.

Evolving Project: This include research projects originated as an idea or to resolve an issue. This can also include a software development project in which requirements might not be known clearly in the beginning and is elaborated as we move ahead and is delivered stage wise.

Customer/supplier project: PRINCE2 is based on a customer/supplier environment. Therefore the customer and supplier can have their own Business Case. By default Business Case refers to the Business Case of the customer. The Business Case is owned by the Executive.

Multi-organization project: Some examples are joint ventures, research and government projects.

The project types discussed above will have their own output, outcome and benefits.

The **output** of a project is the specialist products, the **outcome** is the result of the change derived from using the projects outputs and **benefit** is the measurable improvement resulting from an outcome seen as an advantage by at least one of the stakeholders. Example for a project that involves implementing an ERP to improve operational efficiency the output is ERP itself, the outcome is improvement in operational efficiency. The benefit is the reduction in the cost by 1 million USD per annum due to reduction in wastage.

The focus of business case is to determine whether the expected benefits from the project are, and remains, desirable, viable and achievable. It answers the question, is it worth putting money and efforts in the project?

The Business Case is not a static document, nearing the end of each stage it is reviewed and continually updated with current information to determine if the project remains viable. If the Business Case ceases to be viable, then the project should be changed or stopped.

The diagram below depicts the development path of a business case

BUSINESS CASE PROCEDURE

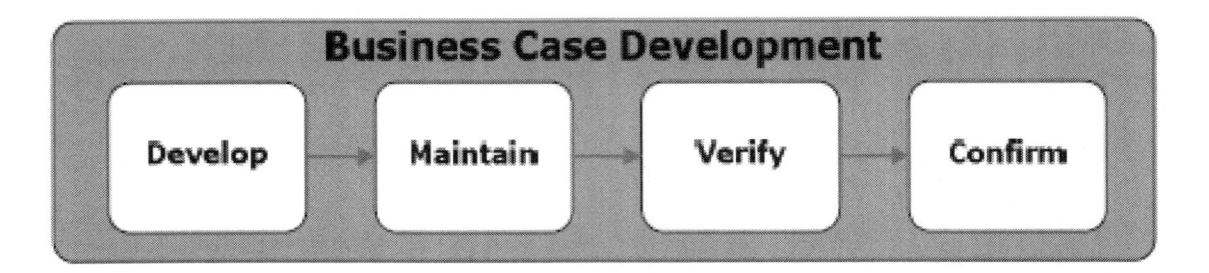

Business Case Development

Develop → Maintain → Verify → Confirm

The outline Business Case is created in the startup stage; it is detailed in initiating a project stage. It is then verified at the critical points during the project, such as at the end of each stage.

The Business Case is developed and maintained as per the following four steps

- Develop
- Verify
- Maintain
- Confirm the Benefits

Develop – Outline Business Case is created based on the project mandate from the corporate program management. The mandate contains an outline of the business case and explains the reason why the project is needed. The mandate triggers the start up stage of the project. The detailed business case is completed near the end of the initiation stage after taking inputs on time scales, cost and product information from the project plan. The detail Business Case is a part of PID.

Verify – The Business Case is verified at all the critical points in the project management lifecycle. Some of these are shared below.

- At the end of the "Starting Up a Project" process. This is the very first process and it plans the Initiation Stage. The Project Board must see the value before they will invest and allow the Initiation Stage to begin.
- At the end of the Initiation Stage (remember the Initiation Phase produces the PID, Project Plan etc…). The Project Board needs to decide whether to authorize the project to start so the first stage can begin.
- This is for the Project Manager during the Controlling a Stage process. Any new issue or risk or change to a risk can affect the Business Case. The Project Manager will always ask if this issue or risk affects the Business Case.
- The Project Manager updates the Business Case if there are changes in project costs, timescales, risks or benefits.
- At the end of each stage and before the next stage, the Project Board decides to release funds for the next stage to start.
- During the Closing a Project process, the Project Manager assesses the performance of the project in reaching its expected outcomes and benefits.
- After the project, a Benefits Review will be performed by someone from Corporate or Program Management.

Maintaining the Business Case

Business Case needs to be kept updated based on the current performance of the project to reflect the actual situation. It may be done when assessing Risks or Issues, or at the end of a stage. For example some of the typical changes can be: increase or reduction of costs, new information on a risk and so on.

So when is a good time to update the Business Case during the project? A good time to update the Business Case is at the end of every stage, as you will have the true cost of the last stage, and perhaps the updated cost of the next stage, along with any information on issues and risk.

In evolving projects, some deliverables may already be put into products and therefore the project will be receiving some of the expected benefits. This information also needs to be added to the Business Case.

Confirm the Benefits

The approach to confirm the benefits is in 4 steps:

- Identification of the benefits by the Senior User. These are documented. These benefits are stored in the Business Case and the Benefits Review Plan.
- Select objective measurements that reliably prove the benefits. Products failing quality tests, x% increase in sales.
- These measurements will enable you to determine if the benefits are realized or not.
- Collect the baselined measures so that they can be used to compare the improvements. Baselined measures refer to recording the current status of the current day.
- For example, with the CRM application, it is possible to record the average amount of time for a client to order today, the cost of handling each order, customer satisfaction survey, and so on.
- Decide how, when and by whom the benefit measures will be collected. I will explain this using the CRM application as example.
    - Example 1: The Account Manager might be responsible for the client survey.
    - Example 2: The Office Manager might provide the information to show the average time for each order.

Most project benefits are realized after the project has been shut down. Consequently, there has to be a process to continue to check the project benefits. The Benefits Review Plan is also used to determine this. It is created by the Project Manager during the Initiation Stage and it is one of the documents that the Project Board should look for before authorizing the project to start.

The Benefits Review Plan may be updated at the end of each stage in the project, as some benefits can be realized during the project and/or new benefits can be identified

Now you may ask who takes ownership of the Benefits Review Plan once the project has stopped, as the Project Manager is no longer available. It usually is someone in Corporate or Program Management. They will ask the Senior User to provide information and evidence to confirm the benefits.

The purpose of the Benefits Review Plan is to identify the benefits and most importantly, to select how the benefits can be measured so that it is possible to show that they have been reached. You can then compare the new results to the current situation, which leads us to the next point, which is to collect the baselined measures.

For example, for the CRM application, we can measure the following and baseline this information:
- Average cost to handle each order by telephone and follow up
- Average time and cost to create sales reports
- Average time providing information to clients about orders and past orders
- Customer satisfaction (take a survey today)

Lastly, the Benefits Review Plan must include information on the expected timeline for these benefits, i.e., when the benefits can be expected and measured, and who will gather the information.

The Senior User Role is responsible for specifying the benefits. After the project is finished and the project team is disbanded, one of the persons responsible from the Senior User Role will be reporting on the realized benefits to the Corporate or Program Management. They have to clearly show that the expected benefits have been reached or provide information otherwise.

- The Executive is responsible to ensure that benefits reviews are planned and executed. These can happen during and after the project.

• The Project Manager reports to the Project Board on any expected benefits that have been realized during the project, and updates the Benefits Review plan. They will also plan the post-project benefits reviews in the last stage of the project.

Business Case - Contents

The Business Case should describe the reasons for the project and includes information on the estimated costs, risks and expected benefits. It should contain the following parts:
• Executive Summary
• Reasons
• Business Options
• Expected Benefits and expected dis-benefits
• Timescale
• Costs
• Investment Appraisal
• Major Risks

Reasons:

The Business Case should say why the project should be done, i.e., the reasons for doing the project. Remember the different types of projects that were discussed earlier.

Example 1: The reason for the CRM application could be reduced costs, increased user satisfaction and increased sales.

Example 2: Another project might be the merging of two departments due to an acquisition. For now there is no need to provide detailed information or figures. The Reasons information should already be included in the project mandate so that you could get the information from it.
Note: The Reasons information can also be further expanded in the Initiation Phase.

Business Options
PRINCE2 teaches that there are always three options to consider concerning any investment. These are:
- Do nothing
- Do the minimum
- Do something

"Do nothing" may seem a bit strange but let me give you an example. Suppose we discover that the benefits of the CRM project will not be reached, as more than 66% of customers will never wish to order online and prefer to use the telephone. Then it is better that we absolutely do nothing. The "do nothing" option should always be the starting one, as the Project Board can compare the fact of doing nothing with other options put forward that would require investment. If you think about it, this is a good idea instead of rushing ahead into every project just to keep people busy.

The "Do the minimum" and "Do something" options would normally require a detailed Business Analysis showing costs, benefits, desire and viability.

Expected Benefits:

- The Business Case should list each benefit and provide information on how tangible and intangible benefits can be measured and when they can be measured.
- An example of an intangible benefit might be happier workers. This can be measured with the help of a survey.
- The Senior User will be responsible for supplying the list of benefits with the necessary information about benefits and the names of the persons who are responsible for each of them. These persons have the responsibility to monitor the benefits and report to the Senior User and Project Manager.
- Remember, the Benefits Review Plan will contain all the information on how to measure the benefits during and after the project.

Expected Dis-Benefits

- According to PRINCE2 a dis-benefit is an outcome that is seen as negative by one or more stakeholders. Another name might be a negative side-effect. For example, with the online CRM application, the clients will now order and track their orders online without ever having contact with administrative personnel from the company. This could have a negative effect as the administrative people in the company communicate less with the customers via telephone.

Timescales

- The Timescales section deals with such matters as when the project is expected to start and end. It will also include when the benefits will be realized and when the project will pay for itself, so it is not just the time of the project.

Costs

- This section provides detailed cost information for the project. It also includes information on ongoing costs in Operations and Maintenance that will start once the project is complete.

Investment Appraisal

This section uses information from both the Costs and Benefits sections. It compares the benefits over a period of time (most likely in years) to the full cost of the project and ongoing maintenance. The Investment Appraisal shows the stakeholders the value of the project. There are many appraisal techniques that you can choose from such as: Net Benefits, Return on Investment, Payback Period, Net Present Value, etc. It is a good idea to use a technique that is used in your company.

Major Risks

There are always risks in each project and the Business Case must contain an overview of these risks. Note that the Risk Register contains more detailed information about these risks. The Project Board will justify the Project based on cost, benefits and risks. The Business Case must contain a summary of the risks and highlight the more major ones.

Business Case: Responsibilities

Corporate or Program Management

- They provide the project mandate, which will most likely include some information on the Business Case.

- The Corporate or Program Management is interested in hearing about the Benefits of the project.

- During the project, the Project Manager will report on the Benefits to the Program Management and will update the Benefits Review Plan.

- And after the project is completed, the Corporate or Program Management will be responsible for the Benefits Review Plan. They have the responsibility of following up to ensure that the benefits have been realized.

Executive

- The Executive is responsible for the Business Case and the Benefits Review Plan during the project.
- The Executive is also responsible to develop a viable Business Case, securing funding for the project and ensuring the project is aligned with corporate strategy.

Senior User

- The Senior User is responsible for specifying the Benefits and then for ensuring that they are realized by the project.
- They are also responsible for ensuring that the products produced by the project deliver the desired outcomes, in other words, that they can be used as expected.

Project Manager

- Project Manager can assist the Executive in preparing the Business Case.
- For each new or revised issue and risk, they will also do Impact Analysis of the Business Case to see if the issue or risk affects the Business Case.
- They also assess the Business Case at the end of each stage, this information is required by the Project Board and they also keep the Benefits Review Plan updated during the project.

Project Assurance

- Project Assurance provides a kind of audit service on each project to check that it is progressing as planned.
- From a Business Case point of view, they can assist in the development of the Business Case and they will monitor the Business Case for external events. Remember, the Project Manager operates inside the project, so they only see internal events.
- Project Assurance also verifies and monitors the Benefits Review Plan.

Organization

This Theme defines and establishes the project's structure of roles and responsibilities. PRINCE2 is based on Customer and Supplier environment; it defines and the set of responsibilities very clearly. Each role may have one person or several people filling it, an individual may fulfill more than one role.

PRINCE2 has a reserved term for the project board, project manager, and some optional roles, and this term is called the Project Management Team. A PRINCE2 project always have three primary categories of stakeholder, and these must always be included if the project is to be successful.

The three primary interests that make up the project board are the Business interest – the Business Case should provide value for money, the User interest – these will use the project's outputs either to realise the benefits, they may operate, maintain or support the project outputs, and these outputs will impact them, and the Supplier interest – these supply the resources and skills to produce a project's products.

There are four levels of a PRINCE2 organization:

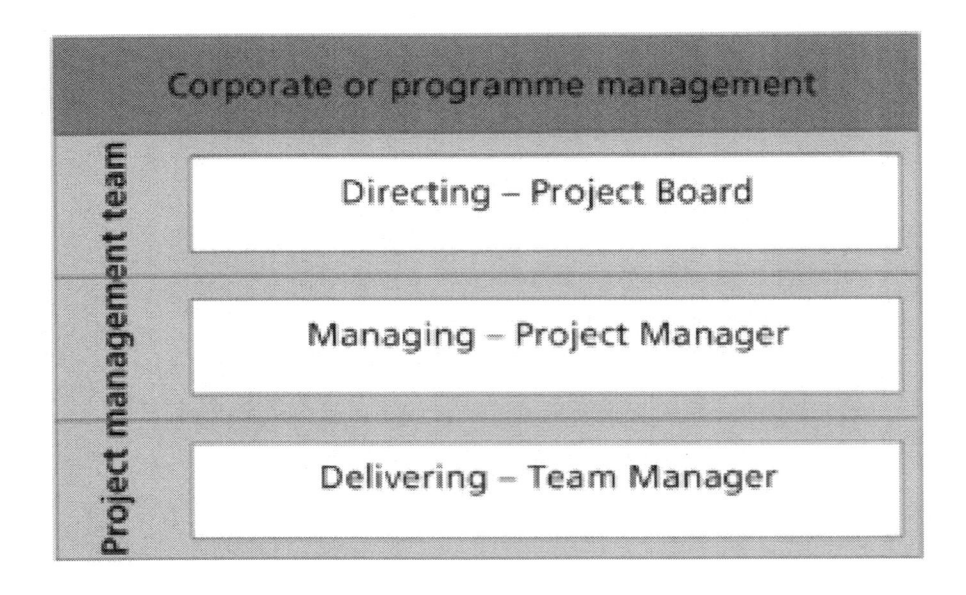

Corporate or programme management
Directing – Project Board
Managing – Project Manager
Delivering – Team Manager

(Project management team encompasses the three lower levels)

1. **Corporate or programme management**, these are outside of the project management team, and are responsible for the Project Mandate, naming the Executive, and defining the project-level tolerances.

2. **The Project Board** is responsible for providing the overall direction and are accountable for the success of the project

3. **The Project Manager** is responsible for the day-to-day management of the project within the constraints laid down by the Project Board.

4. **Team members** are responsible for delivering the project products within quality, time and cost

The **Project Board** responsibilities include being accountable for the success or failure of the project, providing unified direction, providing the resources and authorizing the project funding, and ensuring effective decision-making.

The Project Board should have the right level of authority, be credible, have the ability to delegate, and be available for whenever that decisions and directions are needed.

The Project Board **Executive** is ultimately accountable for the project success and has the veto on any decision making. The executive is responsible for the Business Case.

The **Senior User** role represents those who will use the project's products and also those who will use the products to achieve an objective or deliver benefits. The Senior User specifies the benefits and is held to account by corporate or programme management.

The **Senior Supplier** role represents those who will design, develop, facilitate, procure, and implement the project's products. This role is responsible for the technical integrity of the project.

Each Project Board member is responsible for their own assurance, business, user and supplier. Collectively, this role is called Project Assurance. Each project board member can perform their own project assurance, or they may choose to delegate it.

Project assurance must be independent of the Project Manager and the team and are also responsible for supporting the project manager by giving advice and guidance.

If the project is likely to have many change requests, then the project board during the initiation stage, need to decide whether they have the time to make decisions on these changes, or whether they wish to set up a **Change Authority** who will act upon their behalf.

They would need to agree to 'rules of engagement'.

For example, the project board may only deal with changes above a certain monetary value.

The Project Board may also wish to consider allocating a separate **change budget** to pay for such changes.

The Project Board should not exceed six to eight people otherwise decision-making can be slowed, it is a good idea to consider having off-line supplier and user meetings, and bring a representative back to the project board to act on their behalf..

The **project manager** is responsible for day-to-day management of the project and will delegate responsibility for the creation of products to the team manager or specialist team members themselves.

If the **team manager** is appointed, then the project manager will give the Work Packages to the team manager, and the team manager will give the project manager regular Checkpoint Reports. The Team Manager will therefore perform the daily management of the team members.

Another optional role is the use of **Project Support**. This group will provide administrative services to the project, give advice and guidance on the use of project management tools, and will normally provide configuration management. It project support is not available, and then the project manager will have to do it themselves.

Stakeholder Management

Throughout the project management life cycle a project manager interacts with people and based on the interaction and the decision he takes, the stakeholders become his supporters or blockers. Since a manager has to get things done, having supporters is always good. A sound stakeholder management strategy is helpful in this area. The stakeholders can be categorized based on their interest and influence on the project and based on that an appropriate stakeholder management strategy can be prepared. Power Grid matrix is the tool used for the same.

Classify all the listed stakeholders in the Power / Interest Grid with Stakeholders. The expectations of the stakeholders needs to be met as per below:
- People with High Power and High Interest need to be closely managed as they are the decision makers.
- People with High Power and Low Interest need to be satisfied.
- People with High Interest and Low Power should be kept informed.
- People with Low Interest and Low Power: they require the least amount of attention.

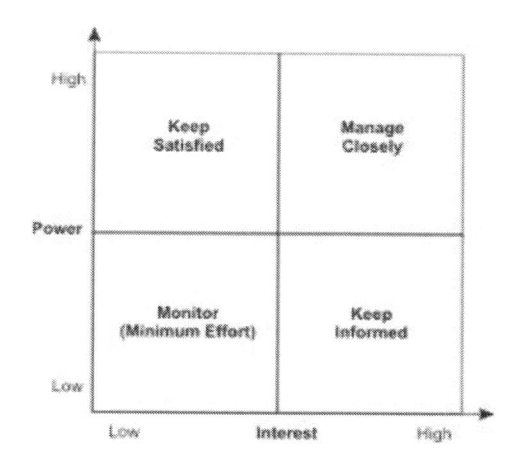

Figure: Power / Interest Grid with Stakeholders

Source: A Guide to the Project Management Body of Knowledge, Fourth Edition (*PMBOK® Guide*) ©2008 Project Management Institute, Inc.
All Rights Reserved.

The communication management strategy

It contains a description of the means and frequency of communication to internal and external stakeholders. In other words it contains what to be sent to whom at what frequency and by what means. The project manager should be responsible for documenting the communication management strategy during initiating a project process. The communication management strategy is reviewed and updated at each stage boundary.

A sample communication plan is shown below

Communication	Format	Frequency	Distribution
Team Briefing	Restricted Intranet	Daily at 9:00	Team and stakeholders with access to secure project info area
Weekly Web Bulletin	Internal Intranet	Weekly	Team, sponsor, senior management
Technical Incident Report	Email	Immediately after Incident	Webmaster, IT Department
Budget and Schedule Detail	Spreadsheets and Detailed Gantt Chart	Bi-Weekly	Sponsor, Senior Management
Accomplishments and Setbacks	Email and Intranet	Weekly	All internal stakeholders
Schedule Milestones	Email and Intranet	Weekly	All internal stakeholders
Cost-to-Date Milestones	Email and Intranet	Weekly	All internal stakeholders
Current Top 5 Risks	Email and Intranet	Weekly	All internal stakeholders

Quality

The focus of PRINCE2 is on the products it creates and these must be fit for purpose so that they will ultimately enable the desired benefits to be achieved. This is product focus ensures that in every project there is a clear understanding of what the project will create in terms of its scope, and the quality criteria for each of the products.

Also PRINCE2 covers the implementation of continuous improvement during the project by striving for more efficiency or effectiveness in both the project's products and its management.

When referring to quality, it may be with regard to any product, a person, a process, a service, or a system that will meet expectations, requirements, specification or stated needs.

To ensure that a plan is accurately scoped, PRINCE2 uses the product based planning technique to create the product breakdown structure and goes on to create their associated Product Descriptions and quality criteria.

Quality management is defined as the coordinated activities to direct and control an organization with regard to quality. A quality management system is the complete set of quality standards, procedures and responsibilities for eyesight or organization.

Because PRINCE2 assumes a customer/supplier environment, then each organization must apply the above.

There are three key aspects to quality within the project:

Quality planning is needed for control and covers definition of the products within the project along with their quality criteria, quality methods and quality responsibilities.

Quality control is reactive, and covers such techniques and activities as quality inspections or testing, and finding ways of eliminating causes of and satisfactory performance. This is where the application of lessons learned can be helpful.

Quality Assurance This must be independent of the project management team and ensure that the project's direction and management remains aligned with relevant corporate or programme management standards and policies. Quality assurance therefore, is all about independently checking that the organization and processes are in place for quality planning and control.

Project Assurance This ensures that the project is being managed appropriately and must be independent of the project manager, project support, team managers and specialists he is. Project assurance is the responsibility of the Project Board.

Quality Register

The results of quality control activities are recorded in a Quality register. A sample quality register is shown below.

Quality Activity ID	Product ID	Product	Quality Method	Producer	Reviewer(s)	Approver(s)	Target Review Date	Actual Review Date	Target Approval Date	Actual Approval Date	Result
1	121	Test Plan	Inspection	Ali	Paulo	John, Rita	14-Feb	21-Feb	21-Feb	28-Feb	Pass
2	124	Water Pump	Performance Test	Paulo	Ali, Bob	John	20-Mar	20-Mar	27-Mar	NA	Fail
3	124	Water Pump	Maintenance Test	Paulo	Ali, Amir	Rita	21-Mar	21-Mar	27-Mar	27-Mar	Pass
.	.	.	.	.	.	.	.	.	.	.	.
.	.	.	.	.	.	.	.	.	.	.	.
9	124	Water Pump	Performance Test	Paulo	Ali, Bob	John	14-Jun		21-Jun		

Quality Review Technique

The PRINCE2 quality review technique is used to assess a product against set quality criteria, and works well for a document walkthrough or analysis of test results.

The quality review technique confirms that the product is complete, ready for approval and that it can be baselined and placed under change control.

The quality review technique consist of the following three steps

- Prepare for Quality Review
- Conduct the Quality Review
- Perform Quality Review Follow - up

Prepare for Quality Review

The various roles that participate in a quality review technique are; Chair, Presenter, Reviewer and Administrator, below are the activities performed by them during a quality review.
- Make administrative arrangements for the review (Chair or Administrator)
- Check that the product is ready for review and confirm reviewer availability (Chair)
- Distribute product copies to reviewers along with the Product Descriptions (Presenter)
- Review the product relative to its quality criteria (Reviewer)
- Submit question list to chair and presenter prior to review (Reviewers)
- Annotate product copy for copy edit errors and return to presenter (Reviewers)
- Produce consolidated question list for the review meeting and send to presenter (Chair)

Conduct the Quality Review

- The following activities are performed when conducting quality review meeting on a PRINCE2 project:
- Introduce attendees and the product being reviewed (Chair)
- Invite reviewers to contribute major questions about the product (Chair)
- Agree actions on each question as it is raised (Review Team)
- Record the actions and responsibilities (Administrator)
- Lead review team through the product and review the consolidated question list (Presenter)
- Agree actions on each question as it is raised (Review Team) Record the actions and responsibilities (Administrator)

Perform the Quality Review Follow –ups

- The following activities are performed to follow up on action items after a quality review meeting has been completed for a PRINCE2 project:
- Coordinate and track the actions (Presenter)
- Sign off on actions as they are completed (Reviewers)
- Sign off on product completion after all actions are complete (Chair)
- Communicate quality review outcome and store quality records (Administrator)
- Request formal approval for the product (Presenter)

Roles and Responsibilities related to Quality Theme

It is the responsibility of **corporate or programme management** to provide the project with details of the organizations quality management system.

The executive of the project board must approve the Quality Management Strategy and the Project Product Description.

The Senior User role must provide the customers with the customer quality expectations and acceptance criteria as well as approving Product Descriptions, resources and the methods for key user aspects. The Senior Supplier role will be responsible for the same items but from the supplier perspective.

The project manager will prepare and document all of the above and ensure that team managers implement the quality control measures agreed in Product Descriptions and Work Packages.

The team manager will ensure that the specialist products are created in line with their Product Descriptions, and keep the Project Manager regularly informed on product quality status.

Project Assurance will assist advice and assure the project board and the project manager on the application and implementation of all quality matters. Project Support will provide administrative support for the quality controls, Quality Register and quality records.

Plan

The purpose of the Plans theme is to provide the following information to all the project team members and thereby facilitate effective communication and control.

- What is required
- How it will be achieved and by whom and details on any specific resource such as specialized hardware or equipment required.
- Details on activities and milestones
- The targets for time, cost, quality, scope, risk and benefits.
- Provides a baseline against which progress can be measured.

A good plan must be viable, desirable and achievable. A project uses the plan as a baseline against which to monitor progress and compare what has actually happened against what was originally planned. Another advantage of creating a plan is that it allows the project manager and team to have a roadmap of what must be done, so that when carrying out the plan there is a greater chance of success.

PRINCE2 uses the rolling wave approach based on progressive elaboration to planning, in a project there is a certain time horizon that we can see clearly, this is called as planning horizon and we can plan in detail for this period and for the time period beyond this we can have a high level plan.

PRINCE2 recommends three levels of planning at project, stage, and optional team plans.

The first plan to be created in PRINCE2 is an initiation stage plan; this plan is created in **starting up a project** process. Later, during the initiation stage the initiating a project process is used to create the project plan which forms the part of the **project initiation documentation (PID)**, and this is used to authorize the project.

Starting with the **initiation stage**, for the subsequent delivery stages, managing a stage boundary process is used to create the next stage plan and this is authorized or otherwise at each end stage assessment.

Optionally, the team manager may create a **team plan** for the delivery of project's products which covers the execution of one or more work packages.

The structure of all PRINCE2 plans is similar for all the levels; however the level of detail will be different at to the project, stage, and team levels. In addition, it important to know that stage plan for the stage is created close to the end of previous management stage to ensure that it contains the latest accurate information

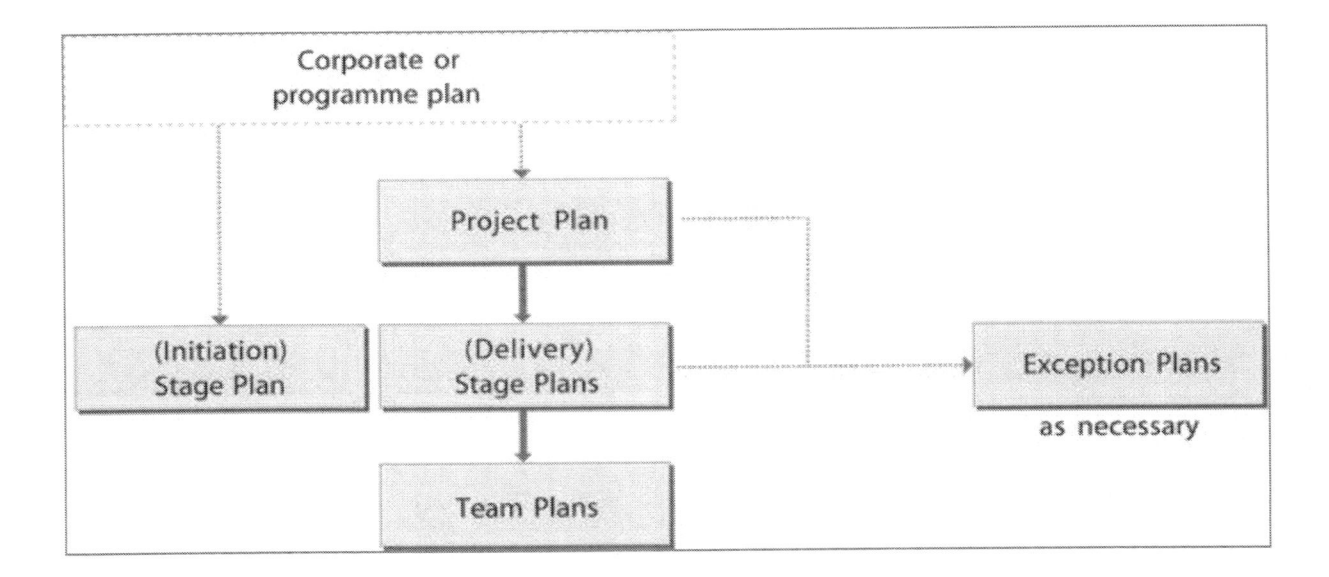

```
Corporate or
programme plan
    │
    ▼
Project Plan ────────────────┐
    │                        │
    ▼                        ▼
(Initiation)   (Delivery)   Exception Plans
Stage Plan     Stage Plans   as necessary
                  │
                  ▼
               Team Plans
```

PRINCE2 uses the principle of **management by exception**. Whenever a plan is forecast to exceed the allowed tolerance, then an **exception report** must be created. If required, an exception plan will now be prepared for the appropriate management level to show the actions required to recover from the effects of a tolerance deviation. If an **exception plan** is approved it will replace the original hence become the new baselined plan (for the project or stage level).

An exception plan at project level must be referred by the **project board** up to corporate or programme management as they alone have the authority to approve such a plan. If the exception plan is to replace the stage plan, then the project board has the authority to approve it. If the project manager has set tolerances at **work package** level, and the team manager is now forecasting that such tolerances will be exceeded, then an issue is raised to bring this to the attention of the project manager, who will determine if this issue can be resolved within stage tolerance levels. If corrective action is needed and approved by the project manager, then this may result by an update to the current work package or authorizing a new work package.

Team managers may create their **team plans** at the same time as the project manager creates the stage plan when preparing for an end stage or an exception assessment. The team plans are used in the **Managing Product Delivery** process.

The **benefits review plan** defines schedule for measurement of the benefits generated from the project's outcome (how and when measurement of the achievement of the project benefits). The benefits review plan is created within the initiating a project process and is a part of PID, and it is updated at each stage boundary. The benefits review plan is used during the closing a project process where it is updated to reflect any benefits that have already been realized, and most importantly those benefits along with the resources that have yet to be realized after the project has been completed.

The product based planning technique.

The use of the PRINCE2 methodology provides powerful benefits over traditional planning approaches. This is because the philosophy is that products are first identified within the planning steps, and only then are the activities, dependencies between them, and the resources required to deliver those projects are than planned. This is called Product-based planning and will be used for project, stage and optionally team plan levels.

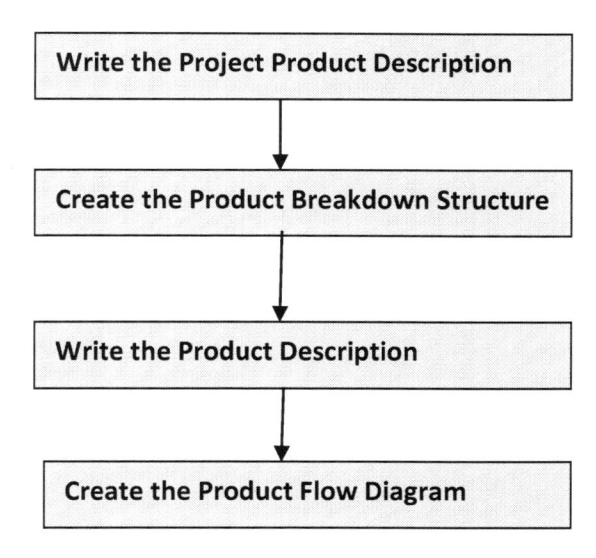

```
┌─────────────────────────────────────────┐
│  Write the Project Product Description  │
└─────────────────────────────────────────┘
                    │
                    ▼
┌─────────────────────────────────────────┐
│  Create the Product Breakdown Structure │
└─────────────────────────────────────────┘
                    │
                    ▼
┌─────────────────────────────────────────┐
│      Write the Product Description      │
└─────────────────────────────────────────┘
                    │
                    ▼
┌─────────────────────────────────────────┐
│     Create the Product Flow Diagram     │
└─────────────────────────────────────────┘
```

Like most planning procedures, this one is iterative in nature and will often be progressively elaborated as the process of creating the plan proceeds. At the end of each stage for example, the project plan will be updated and normally refined. Whenever work on a plan is needed, the **Product-based planning technique** will be used.

At the start of any PRINCE2 project, decisions must be made about how the plan can be passed presented, which will be used, and any specific presentation and layout rules that should be adhered to. If the project is part of a programme them the above may need to use their preferred approach.

Other decisions that need to be made at this point for plans within a project may include any company standards or the use of a planning to all such as Microsoft project. Estimating methods may also be mandated all recommended and will be based on the size, complexity, risk, or preferences within the organization or industry.

The Product-based planning technique consists of four steps, with the first step of writing the project product description only being used for the project plan. The remaining three steps are to create the **product breakdown structure (PBS)**,

Create the lower level product descriptions, and then create the **product flow diagram (PFD)**.

The remaining steps to create the plan document (which starts with identifying activities and dependencies), occurs after the Product-based planning technique, but of course is used in the creation of any PRINCE2 plan.

I shall now describe the sequence from the start of the Product-based planning technique through to final documentation of a given plan:

Write the project product description.
This is the first step, and although the senior user is responsible for specifying the project product, it will often be created by the project manager in close communication with both the senior user and the executive of the project board.

The project product description describes the purpose of the project product and who will use it. It also contains the specialist skills required along with the **customer's quality expectations and the acceptance criteria**/tolerances/acceptance method/exceptions responsibilities.

Create the product breakdown structure (PBS)

This is a hierarchical diagram where the major products of the plan are broken down to the required level of detail. A powerful way creating this is by the use of Post-It notes within a team brainstorming session.

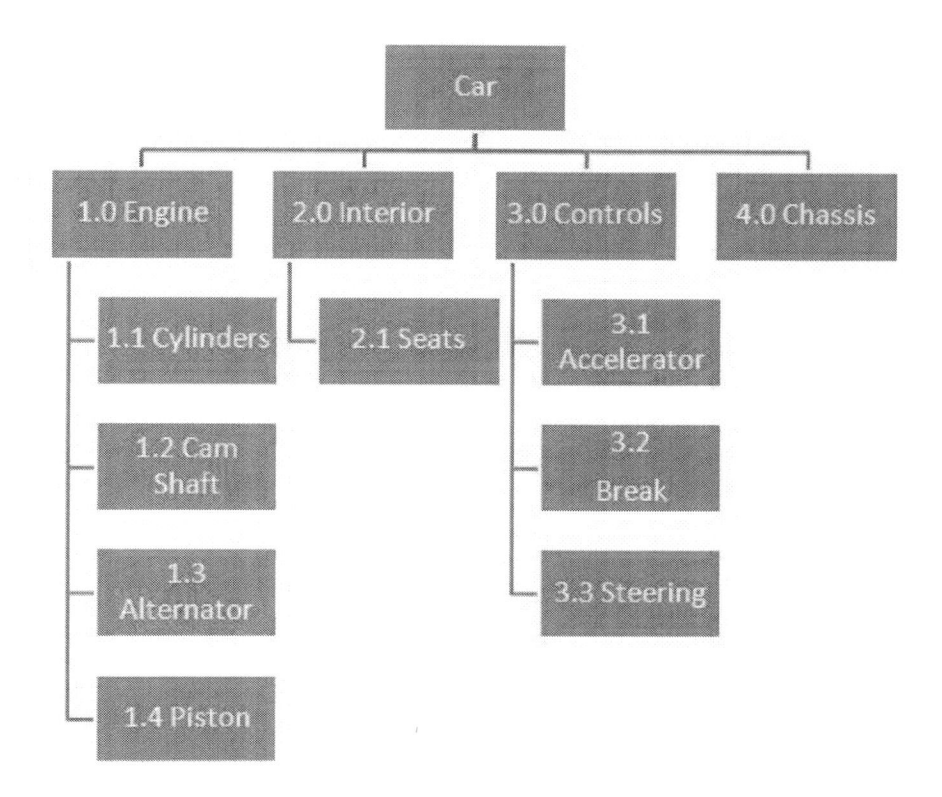

```
                          Car
        ┌──────────┬──────────┬──────────┐
    1.0 Engine  2.0 Interior 3.0 Controls 4.0 Chassis
        │          │          │
    1.1 Cylinders 2.1 Seats  3.1 Accelerator
        │                     │
    1.2 Cam Shaft            3.2 Break
        │                     │
    1.3 Alternator           3.3 Steering
        │
    1.4 Piston
```

There are rules for constructing a PBS. A lower level product can be a component of only one higher level product. The PBS does not show sequence, and therefore the only linkages between each product must either be upwards or downwards, in other words there must be no loops or sequencing. Whenever breaking a product into lower level products, there must always be at least two lower level products, since a 1 to 1 link would infer that the higher product consists entirely of the lower product – and hence they must be the same product!
It is important to differentiate any **external products** required within a plan, and these are defined as any product that already exists or that they must be created or updated outside the scope of this particular plan (however these products are required in order to create one or more of the plans products). An example might be that a plot of land requires planning permission from the local authority before building can start work. The external product here would be 'planning permission granted'.

External products will normally be seen as a risk because they are outside of the control of the project and hence each external product should be entered on the **risk register** along with appropriate responses.

Another concept which is important here is that the products may have different 'states' and that it is important to differentiate these from each other within the plan. For example in a relocation project, you may need to dismantle a Computer System, deliver it to the new site, and then install it. Because each of these **product states** are unique and would need associated activities and resources, then it is important to include these within the plan. In this example they could be described as 'dismantled system', 'delivered system', and 'installed system'.

Since the Product-based planning technique will be used for each level of plan, then the lower levels of a PBS at project level will become the higher levels of product at the appropriate stage plan level.

At this point in the sequence, only the project product description will have been created. The next step is to focus on product descriptions at the lower levels within the PBS.

Write the product descriptions.

For each product shown on the PBS, a **product description** is required, and should be created as soon as possible after the need for the product has been identified. Once a plan is baselined after approval by the appropriate authority, then all included product descriptions are also baselined and hence under change control.

PRINCE2 recommends involvement by the users in the drafting of product descriptions. If similar product descriptions have been used in previous projects or stages, then these may be available via a library often looked after by project support. Each product description must include the **quality criteria** against which is the product is designed and ultimately authorized, and it is important to give this criteria careful thought as it alone differentiates unacceptable product from an unacceptable one at a **quality review**

Create the product flow diagram.

Unlike the PBS, a product flow diagram (PFD) identifies and defines the sequence in which the products of the plan will be developed and also shows the link dependencies between them. Again such diagrams are best created using Post-It notes within a team or brainstorming workshop.

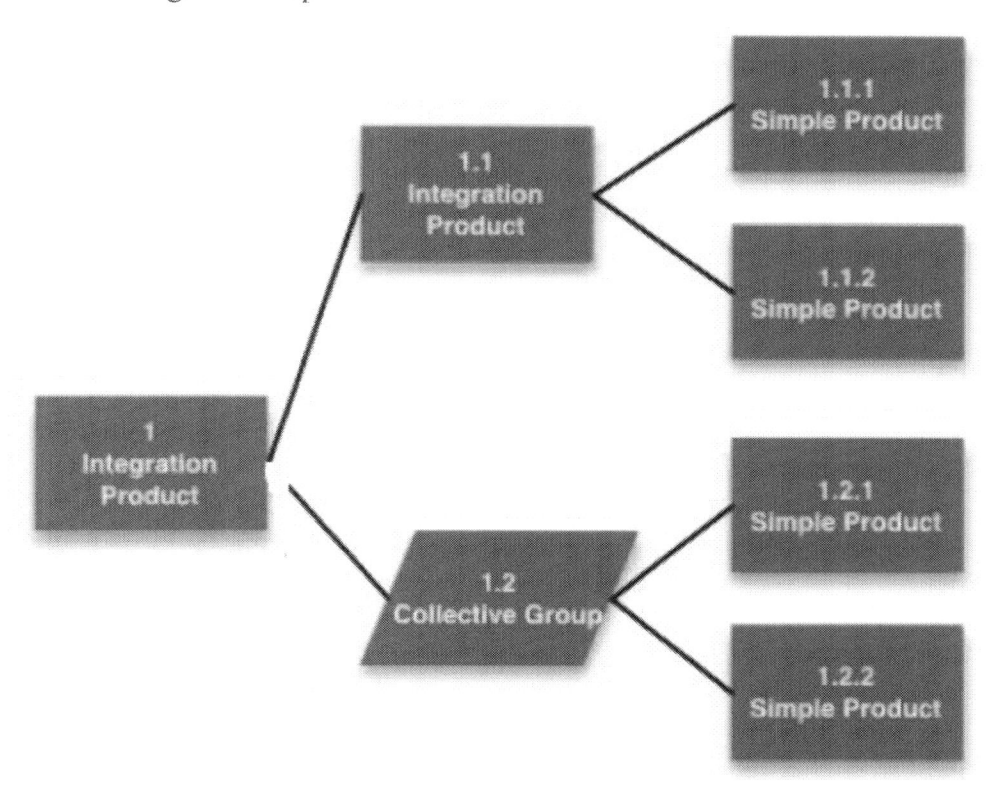

This is the final step within the **Product-based planning technique**, however the plan document has yet to be completed, and I will now cover the remaining steps to do this:

Identify activities and dependencies.

It is tempting just to include the activities required to create the projects products. But this would be a mistake since such activities must also include management activities including communication, along with quality checking, and authorizing activities for each product. Dependencies between each activity and appropriate products must now be identified and these will include both **internal and external dependencies**. Internal dependencies reflect logical relationships between each activity, for example activity B cannot start until activity

A has finished. An example of an external dependency might be the release of a product by an independent third party that is required by this project at a certain point within it.

Prepare estimates.

There are many **estimating techniques** that can be used, but the objective of estimating is that for each activity it is known how long it will take, the resource knowledge and skills required, the amount of work effort to carry out the activity, and any non human resources such as facilities or tools.
Methods that can be used for estimating include:

Top-down estimating where the overview of a plan is broken down into detailed through the levels of the product breakdown structure, so that no and ratios between development phases such as design and testing can be proportioned accordingly.

Bottom-up estimating. As the name suggests estimating is down at the lowest level within both activities and products and can be summed upwards to arrive at the total estimate.

Comparative and parametric estimating. The former depends upon date or stage from previous and similar projects in terms of both products and activities, and the latter is basing estimates and measured/empirical data.

Three-point estimating. Rather than use a single point of estimate, that is, just using a best guess, this involves asking for a best case estimate, at most likely place estimate, and a worst case estimate. The final step is to use a formula such as adding the best case to the worst case plus three times the most likely estimate, and dividing the result by six.

Prepare the schedule.
This is the generation of a bar chart or Gantt chart showing the activities, then dependencies, and the sequence in which they must be performed. **Critical path analysis** is normally used here, and hence the identification of critical and non-critical activities to determine the earliest project finish date along with the critical path and the client or slack of non-critical activities.
Note that the critical path by definition as zero **float or slack**, whereas non-critical activities will have some amount that determines the amount of time that such an activity can slip or extend without affecting future activities or the end date of the project.

Assess and assign resources.

The first step here is to identify who is available in terms of knowledge skills and experience, to carry out the work. This will also include the identification of available non human resources such as facilities.
The next steps is to assign such resources to each appropriate activity, taking into consideration work effort estimates and that their availability. As a consequence of this the critical path may be modified.

Resource Leveling

There are two situations which may now be present; the first is that large resource peaks will be evident at certain points within the project, and this can result in management or logistical problems. The second may result in over utilization of some resources. The act of resolving either of the above is called **leveling**. The **critical chain technique** may also be helpful at this step.

Agree control points.

By now, a draft schedule would have been created for the plan and key **plan control points** need to be identified. These will include at project plan level, the end stage points, and that stage plan level, control points such as product completion, quality checking, and authorization or audit points.

Define milestones.

The definition of a milestone is a zero duration activity, and similar to the above, shows key control points. Such **milestones** may highlight key review points or early indication of issues, as well as indicating completion of key aspects within the plan.

Calculate total resource requirements and costs.
It is at this point for the first time, that resource requirements and other costs can be calculated to produce the planned as **budget**. Such a budget must include the cost of the management and specialist activities, any optional risk or change budgets, and the cost tolerances.

Present the schedule.

A project schedule can be presented in the form of **Gantt charts**, Project Network Diagrams, or an excel sheet. PRINCE2 also includes a management document called the **product checklist**, which basically is a list of the major products plus key dates in their delivery within a particular plan. Such dates may include draft product ready, planned quality check, and approval.

Analyze the risks.
This activity will run in parallel with all the other steps as **risks** may be identified at any point during the creation or update of a given plan. The main purpose here is having identified risks, their responses and associated resources are built into the plan so that the **risks can be managed**. By the very act of planning new risks may consist of those related to the plan itself or the information contained within it.

Document the plan.
This is the final step and leads to the creation of the complete **plan document**. Aspects that need to be included here will include the schedule, the costs, the required controls and supporting text which will be added here to explain the plan, any constraints on it, external dependencies and assumptions, monitoring and can trolling activities along with risk responses.

Roles and Responsibilities related to the plan theme

Corporate Programme management set project tolerances and are responsible for approving Exception plan when project-level tolerance are forecast to be exceeded.

Executive approves the project plan and defines tolerance for each stage and approve the stage plan. Approves the Exception plan when stage –level tolerance are forecast to be exceeded. Commit business resources to the stage plan

Senior User ensures that project plan and stage plans remain consistent from the user perspective and commit user resources to stage plans

Senior Supplier ensures that project plan and stage plans remain consistent from the supplier perspective and commit supplier resources to stage plans

Project Manager prepares the project plan and stage plans and decides how the management and technical stages are to be applied. Defines the work package level tolerance and instruct corrective action when the work package level tolerance are forecast to exceed.

Team Manager prepares the team plans and prepares schedules for each work package

Project Assurance monitors changes to the project plan to see whether there is any impact on the project business case.

Project Support assists with the compilation and the distribution of plans

Risk

A Risk is a known unknown that impact the outcome of the project negatively or positively. A key responsibility of a project manager is to continuously anticipate risk and respond to them so that they are not converted into issues. Effective management of risks prevents them from turning into issues and this is the primary aim of risk theme. The risk management involves the process of identifying, assessing planning and implementing the risk response plan. The risks in a project keep on changing based on the implementation of the risk response, so the risk management should continue for the entire project life cycle. The risks are captured in the document called as risk register.

The risks can be positive as well as negative. The positive risks are based on opportunities and strengths; however the negative risks are based on weakness and threats. One common point for both opportunities and threats is the word uncertainty, the only difference is that you would want to reduce the probability and impact of threats, and enhance the probability and impact of opportunities.

The first step in the risk management within a project is to adopt and tailor the organization's risk management strategy which describes how risk management will be implemented. In addition an understanding of an organization's risk appetite towards risk taking (risk seeker, risk averse or risk neutral) must be understood, and this will culminate within a PRINCE2 project by the creation of the risk management strategy document laying out how risk should be managed by this particular project. This forms part of the project initiation documentation developed during the Initiating a Project process.

The first PRINCE2 process that is used is starting up a project, and this is triggered by the project mandate being issued by corporate or programme management. This should include any known risks at that point in time. The daily log is created here, and used as a temporary 'risk register' to capture and manage any known pre-project risks. New and modified risks will be added during starting up a project as the project approach and project brief is created including creation of the outline business case, and when creating the plan for the initiation stage.

During the initiating a project process, the risk register is created at the same time as the risk management strategy and any outstanding risks within the daily log are now transferred to the newly created risk register. The Business case is now refined into the detailed business case and the business case contents includes a summary of the main business risks. This register contains a set of details on each threat and opportunity, the probability and impact assessment, quantitative assessment, risk response plan and details on risk review.

During the delivery stage, the risk responses are implemented, monitored and controlled. The responsibility for this lies with the project manager. Throughout the project life cycle existing risk may change in terms of their probability or impact and the new risks may arise. Whenever an issue (problem, concern, request for change, off-specification) is raised, as part of issue evaluation, their impact on project risks should be determined because this may change existing risks or create new ones.

At the end of each stage, using the managing a stage boundary process, new risks may come to light as part of assessing the existing stage and preparing the plan for the next stage.

The PRINCE2 procedure for risk management is summarized as follows;

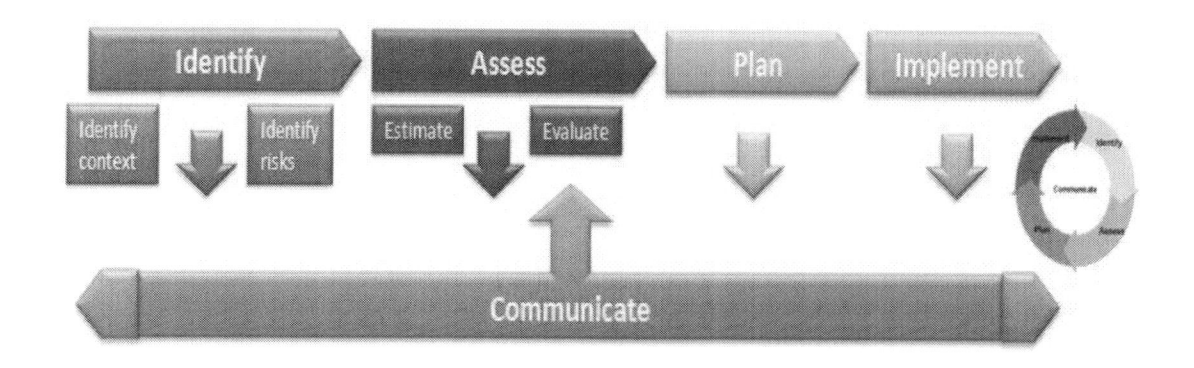

Identify. First the context of the project is determined to understand the specific objectives that are at risk, and develop the risk management strategy. Now all the threats and opportunities are identified and are entered along with early warning indicators, onto the risk register.

There are many ways to identify risks and these include brainstorming techniques, risk workshops, use of risk prompt and checklists, the use of lessons from previous projects, and a risk breakdown structure, which is decomposition as per the category of risk, For Example Technical Risks, Manpower Risks, Requirements Risk and Schedule Risks and so on.

Assess. The qualitative risk analysis is done by determining the probability (Likely hood of happening) and impact of the risks. Based on the multiplication of these two factors urgency of the risk is decided and risk profiling is done as shown below.

Probability and Impact Matrix

		*Impact	Very Low	Low	Medium	High	Very High	Very High	High	Medium	Low	Very Low
		Probability	0.05	0.10	0.20	0.40	0.80	0.80	0.40	0.20	0.10	0.05
Very High	71-90%	0.90	0.05	0.09	0.18	0.36	0.72	0.72	0.36	0.18	0.09	0.05
High	51-70%	0.70	0.04	0.07	0.14	0.28	0.56	0.56	0.28	0.14	0.07	0.04
Medium	31-50%	0.50	0.03	0.05	0.10	0.20	0.40	0.40	0.20	0.10	0.05	0.03
Low	11-30%	0.30	0.02	0.03	0.06	0.12	0.24	0.24	0.12	0.06	0.03	0.02
Very Low	up to 10%	0.10	0.01	0.01	0.02	0.04	0.08	0.08	0.04	0.02	0.01	0.01

(Columns 4-8: Threats; Columns 9-13: Opportunities)

Qualitative Risk Analysis Matrix

Likelihood	Insignificant	Minor	Moderate	Major	Severe
Almost certain	M	H	H	E	E
Likely	M	M	H	H	E
Possible	L	M	M	H	E
Unlikely	L	M	M	M	H
Rare	L	L	M	M	H

(Columns 2-6: Consequences)

After the risk profiling is done. The quantitative risk analysis is conducted for high priority risks only as it is an expensive process. Techniques such as expected monetary value analysis, decision tree and sensitivity analysis using tornado diagrams can be used for quantitative risk analysis.

Plan. This is where appropriate responses for each of the threats and opportunities are identified in order to reduce the former and maximize the latter. Following are the strategies for negative and the positive risks.

Avoid. This entails taking some action upfront and hence changing some aspect of the project such that the risk probability becomes zero and/or there will be no impact. For example, if there is a schedule risk due to aggressive timelines in a project, renegotiating the timelines with the customer and get his acceptance on the relaxed timelines and thereby eliminating any schedule related risks.

Reduce. Another term for this is mitigating the risk and unlike avoid, taking action to reduce will either reduce probability of happening or impact of the risk. For example; if there is a schedule risk due to aggressive timelines of an activity, assigning this activity to a highly skilled resource. This will definitely reduce the risk of slippage; however will not eliminate it completely.

Transfer. The risk is transferred to a third party by making it or responsible for all or some of the financial impact of the risk, and this is normally done in the form of contract clauses that come into force as a result of such a risk. Buying Insurance policy is an example of transferring the risk.

Accept. This means taking no response action. This is usually the response strategy if severity of the risk is less than the cost or complexity of implementing a response action. Such threats must be continually monitored to ensure that the accept response remains tolerable, and if not, then one of the other responses should be substituted.

Fallback. This is also called as contingency planning and is different to the first three in that no action is taken up front. This is a reactive approach and entails creating a fallback plan with actions to be implemented only if the risk occurs. For Example a business continuity and disaster recovery plan.

For the response plans mentioned above **a Risk budget** is kept aside which is a sum of money included within the project budget but set aside to fund the specific management responses to the project threats and opportunities. Although this could be appropriate for any of the responses, it is particularly useful for when fallback is used, since it will only be implemented should the linked risk actually occur. If such a budget is to be used then both the amount and how it is to be used should be documented within the risk management strategy document.

The responses for an opportunity are:

Exploit. This entails taking some action upfront that will seize the opportunity ensuring that it will occur and that the positive impact will be realized. This strategy seeks to eliminate the uncertainty associated with a particular positive risk by making the opportunity happen. Examples of exploit are; to assign highly skilled and experienced resources on the project to ensure that project is delivered before the planned time, enhancing the capacity of manufacturing capacity by upgrading the existing facility or creating a new one.

Enhance. Enhancing a risk involves identifying the root cause of a positive risk so that you can influence the root cause to increase the probability of happening of the positive risk. For example, in order for you to get a business opportunity, your workforce needs to have substantial skills in a particular technology. You can enhance the positive risk (opportunity) by training your workforce on that particular technology or hiring technology specialists. Hence, the probability of you getting the deal is increased. Another example would be due to increasing awareness of diabetes through various campaigns the people who are prone to diabetes or having high sugar levels may stop eating Chocolate candies, a company that is into this business may decide to come out with sugar free candy to enhance the risk.

Reject. It also means you are acknowledging that you'd rather not Exploit, Share, or Enhance the risk. This is normally chosen much like the accept response to threats, that is, because it is not economical to take such an action. In a similar way, the reject response should be monitored to ensure it remains the best choice for this individual opportunity, and a different response chosen if required.

Share. This can be used for both, negative risk (threat) or a positive risk (opportunity) type of risk. These responses will be included as part of creating the next stage plan or exception plan. This response is a form of risk sharing between two or more parties and is normally built into a contract. It uses some form of a pain/gain formula, and prescribed limits are used between the parties that divide up either the financial pain or gain if the opportunity or threat does not materialize.

Implement. The risk responses identified above, are now implemented, and how effective each response is will be monitored and corrected where necessary to achieve the desired effect.

Communicate. Unlike the first four sequences above, this is a parallel and ongoing activity to ensure that information on all of the threats and opportunities are communicated both internally and externally to the project. The risks are generally communicated through time driven reports (such as Highlight Report, Checkpoint Report and so on) and event driven reports (such as end Stage report, end Project report and so on).

Roles and Responsibilities related to Risk theme are:

Corporate or Programme Management provides the corporate level policy for the risks

Executive is responsible for ensuring that the risk management strategy exists and the risks associated with the Business case are identified, assessed and controlled.

Senior User is responsible for ensuring that risks related to users are identified, assessed and controlled.

Senior Supplier is responsible for ensuring that risks relating to supplier aspects are identified, assessed and controlled.

Project Manager creates the Risk Management Strategy, creates and maintains the risk register. Ensures that the project risks are identified, assesses and controlled throughout the lifecycle of the project.

Team Manager participates in the identification, assessment and control of risks at Work Package level.

Project Assurance review risk management practices to ensure that they are performed in alignment with the project's Risk Management Strategy

Project Support assists the project maintaining the project's risk register

Change Theme

The PRINCE2 Manual uses the Change Theme to describe how change control should be executed. All changes are dealt with as a type of project issue. An issue can be

1. General issues
2. Request for Change
3. Off Specifications.

General issues

First of all, any general issue could be dealt with 'face-to-face' if appropriate - logging it as a 'formal' project issue would be done if that were the best and only option. As an example, 'general' issues could include:

- A question or query
- A good idea or a suggestion
- An observation
- A concern

Request for Change.

This is a change requested from the Customer/User side, and would, if implemented, cause a change to what had been originally agreed, to the Acceptance Criteria, Specifications/Scope. It might be a request to add or subtract to the original agreement. If you were having a house built, two examples might be you requesting an extra bathroom, or asking for a dividing wall to be removed. As such, any extra costs relating to this change should be paid for by the Customer/Users.

Off Specification

This covers errors or omissions either in work already carried out, or planned for the future. This will result in NOT being able to meet the originally agreed Acceptance Criteria, Specification/Scope.

An example similar to above would be if the builder of your new house advises that they can't include your patio area within the price. As such, any extra costs (either in re-work to fix the off-specification, or reducing the price to you), should be met by the builder. Suppose that (possibly in order to meet your timescale...) you agreed to accept what the builder could give you (that is, house without the patio), then in PRINCE2 terms, this is called a CONCESSION.

Request for Change/Off Specification management.

If either an RFC or Off Specification would cause forecasted Tolerance to be exceeded - then the Project Manager MUST bring this to the Project Board's attention by raising an Exception Report.

If the change is an Off Specification, the project manager would try to fix the problem using any available Tolerance (although optionally it may be prudent to seek advice from the Project Board...)

But if the change is a Request for Change, the Project Manager MUST bring this to the attention of the Project Board - whether or not the change can be done within Tolerance. If the RFC can be done within Tolerance, the Project Manager would use the Directing a Project activity "Give Ad-Hoc Direction, as the means of communicating this.
The Project Board are usually senior people, and they may consider that having to authorize (or not), all changes, that they should not be involved. In such a case, they may delegate their responsibilities to a "Change Authority". This authority will act on the board's behalf. Another possibility is that the Change Authority only handle lower priority/impact issues - say for example, under a certain cost, and the Project Board deal with all the rest.

Another option (to be discussed during the Initiation Stage, and included in the Project Plan), is to include a Change Budget in addition to the Project Budget. This has the added advantage of ensuring that changes do not "eat" into cost Tolerance.

If such a budget is not made available, then any changes beyond budget or Project Tolerance would require the Board to seek agreement from Corporate (or Programme) Management - since it was they that set Project Tolerance. PRINCE2 states quite rightly, that Project Issues should not be considered in isolation. This will greatly enhance decision-making.

Each issue should be considered in the light of any impact to the Business Case, Risks, Cost, Time - and should be carefully weighed against any such benefit, advantage or saving. Remember also, that if a product is to be changed, its Product Description should be checked to see if that too, needs changing.

All issues when raised should be entered into the Issue Log and categorized. All issues should be given a priority rating (i.e. Must Have, Nice to have and so on). After Imapct Analysis the Priority may have to be reconsidered by the Project Manager or Project Board.

Any issues that are simple misunderstandings should be dealt with directly and the Issue Log updated to reflect this. For all other types, an Impact Analysis must be carried out.

The Impact Analysis covers:
- What would have to change and what work effort it would take
- What the impact would be on all plans (Team, Stage, Project), and whether this would cause deviation beyond Tolerance
- What the impact would be on the Business Case and risks

Remember that the impact may be positive or negative (the Business Case might be improved as a result of the issue!)

One final point. Whenever considering issue action, the Project Board (or their delegated Change Authority), have the following options:

Agree to the change
Agree to the change being implemented (possibly by approving an Exception Plan if the change would have caused the original Plan to exceed Tolerance)

Reject the change

For Request for Changes, decide not to implement - but keep it "live" by placing it in "pending" on the Issue Log. This might be implemented later or not at all.
They may remove the cause of the issue - thus remedying the need to resolve the issue itself
They may decide to prematurely close the project

Roles and Responsibilities related to the change theme are;

Corporate Programme Management provides the corporate level strategy for change control, issue resolution and configuration management

Executive determines the change authority and the change budget, sets the severity ratings and priority for issues, respond to request for advice from the project manager and make decision on escalated issues with the focus primarily on continual business justification.

Senior User takes decision on escalated issues with the primary focus on safeguarding the expected benefits.

Senior Supplier takes decision on escalated issue with primary focus on safeguarding the integrity of the complete solution

Project Manager manages the configuration management procedure, manages issue and change control procedure, creates and maintain the issue register

Team Manager implements corrective actions for Work Package level issues

Project Assurance advises on examining and resolving issues

Project Support maintains the configuration item records, produces product status account and assists the project manager to maintains the issue registers

Progress Theme

Purpose

- To establish how to monitor and then to compare actual achievements against those planned during the project life cycle.

- To provide a forecast for the project objectives and the project's continued viability.

- To be able to control any unacceptable deviations.

- Progress is about checking progress compared to the plan, checking project viability and controlling any deviations.

Principles represented in the Progress Theme?

Three of the seven principles are represented in the Progress Theme; they are:

• Manage by stages: the Project Board is to use stages as a control point.

• Continued business justification, as the Business Case is continually checked that the project is still worth doing.

• Managed by Exception. Where tolerances are used, refer certain issues up to the next management level.

Another PRINCE2 principle is that projects are managed by exception, setting tolerances for project objectives to establish limits of delegated authority. Tolerances define the amount of discretion that each management level can exercise without the need to refer up to the next level for approval. The Progress theme provides the mechanisms to monitor progress against the allowed tolerances, and the controls to escalate to the next level should any forecast suggest that one or more tolerances will be exceeded.

If there is an exception that can impact stage level tolerances the approval authority is Project Board.

If there is an exception that can impact project level tolerances the approval authority is Corporate Program Management.

Progress, Progress Controls, Exceptions and Tolerances

What is Progress?

Progress is checking and controlling where you are compared to the plan. This is done for the Project Plan, Stage Plan and Work Package.

What are Progress Controls?

Progress Controls are used by one layer to monitor the progress of the layer below it. For instance, the Project Board is to monitor the progress of Project Manager or Project Manager to monitor the progress of the Teams that create the products. The layer above can do the following:

• Monitor actual progress against plans

• Review plans with forecast

• Detect problems and identify risks

• Initiate corrective action to fix issues

• Authorize further work to be done. Example: The Project Board can authorize a next stage and a Project Manager can authorize a new Work Package.

What are Exceptions and Tolerances?

An Exception is a situation where it can be forecast that there will be a deviation beyond the agreed tolerance levels. Tolerances are the deviation above and below a plan's target.

For example, the project should take 6 months, with a tolerance of ±1 month. Tolerance levels could also be set for all six tolerance areas, i.e., Time, Cost, Quality, Scope, Benefits and Risk.

Question: What would be the result if Tolerance were not used in a project between the Project Board and the Project Manager levels?

Answer: In that case, every small issue that would occur, the Project Manager would escalate to the Project Board and they would end up working on the project 8 hours a day and therefore would be doing a lot of work for the Project Manager.

Remember the Project Board are busy people and we don't want the project to take up much of their time. Setting tolerances allows the Project Manager to handle smaller issues and only bother the Project Board for bigger issues (more efficient use of time for Project Board)

Remember the Project Board are busy people and we don't want the project to take up much of their time. Setting tolerances allows the Project Manager to handle smaller issues and only bother the Project Board for bigger issues that are outside the specified tolerance.

Tolerance Example: A 6-month project with a tolerance of ±1 months. If the project is forecast to be 1 week late, the Project Manager would deal with this and not escalate it. But if the project is forecast to be two months late, then they would escalate it to the Project Board.

When are the Six Tolerances set?

Let us look at when tolerances can be decided on:

• **Time and Cost Tolerances**: These are decided in the Project Plan, Stage Plans and Work Packages.

• **Scope Tolerances:** Decided in Project Plan, Stage Plan and Work Packages. Note: Scope changes would require change control.

• **Risk tolerances** will be first defined in the Risk Management Strategy document and the Project Board can change risk tolerance for the Stage Plan. The Project Manager may change risk tolerances for the Work Package.

• **Quality Tolerances** are defined in the Project Product Descriptions and the Product Descriptions, as Quality is related to the products.

• **Benefits tolerances** are defined only in the Business Case and this is kept up to date during the project. The Benefits are also defined in the Business Case

Management Stages and Technical Stages

Why are Management Stages used as controls by the Project Board?

Management stages are partitions of the project with decisions points for the Project Board between each stage. A management stage is a collection of activities to produce products and is managed by the Project Manager.

Why are Management Stages important for the Project Board?

• They provide review and decision points at end of each stage and before the next stage.

- They can check the viability of the project.
- They can authorize one stage at a time, or choose to stop the project.
- They review the End Stage Report of the last stage and Review plan for next stage.
- Then can check project progress compared with baselined Project Plan at the end of each stage.

As you can see, stages are important for the Project Board. Also, with the help of tolerance, the Project Board can give the day-to-day authority of running the stage to the Project Manager. The Project Manager sends regular highlight reports to inform them how well the stage is going according to the Stage Plan and does not otherwise bother them unless the stage goes or is forecast to go out of tolerance.

How many stages should be in a project?

The minimum number of stages in a PRINCE2 project is two: the Initiation Stage to define and agree what needs to be done, and at least one other stage to produce the products.

How to decide the number of stages?

This depends on a number of items and as you can see, it's a bit of a balancing act. Start by considering the following:

- How far ahead is it sensible to plan?

- Where do key decision points have to be made in the project? (Example: Maybe after creating a prototype or after completion of a major part of the product. This would be a good point for stage end.)

- The amount of risk and the complexity in a project. (If similar to another project, then there will be less.). Higher the risk and complexity more will be the number of management stages.

The number of management stages in a project, and is a bit of balancing act as the more number of management stages provide better control on the project, however increases the administrative overhead.

11.8 What are Technical Stages?

Technical stages are a way of grouping work. The best way to understand this is to look at how they differ from Management Stages.

- **Technical stages can overlap but management stages do not.**

- Technical stages are usually linked to specialist skills (e.g., Requirements Analyses and Design Product, while Management Stages are more focused on business justification and authority to spend).

- A technical stage can span a management stage boundary.

- A management stage can have more than one technical stage.

Roles and Responsibilities related to Progress theme

Corporate programme management provides the project tolerances and the document them in project mandate and make decisions related to exceptions when project – level tolerance is forecast to exceed.

Executive provides stage level tolerances and makes decision when stage level tolerances are forecast to be exceeded. Ensures that progress towards the outcome remain consistent from business perspective. Recommend future action on the project to corporate or programme management if the project tolerance is forecast to be exceeded

Senior User ensures that progress towards the outcome remain consistent from user perspective.

Senior Supplier ensures that progress toward the outcome is consistent from the supplier perspective

Project Manager authorizes the Work Package level tolerances and monitor progress against the stage plan. Produces highlight reports, End Stage report, lesson report and end project report. Produce exception reports when the stage level tolerances are forecast to be exceeded.

Team Manager agrees on work package with the project manager, produce checkpoint reports and notify the project manager of any forecast deviation from work package tolerance.

Project Assurance review and verify the business case against the external events, verify impact on the business case on the basis of progress or due to change in the plan.

Project Support assist with the compilation and distribution of reports, assist the project manager in maintaining the issue and risk registers.

Chapter 6 – Management Products

26 Management Products Found in a PRINCE2 Project:

Management Product	Description
Benefits Review Plan	Defines how and when measurement of project benefits achievement can be made
Business Case	Provides justification for the project in terms of benefits, costs, risks, and timescales and is used to assess viability
Checkpoint Report	Reports Work Package progress and information from the Team Manager or team to the Project Manager
Communication Management Strategy	Describes the means and frequency of communication between the project and its stakeholders
Configuration Item Record	Describes the status, version, variants and relationships for a configuration item (product, product component or release)
Configuration Management Strategy	Defining how and by whom the project's products (each a configuration item) will be controlled and protected
Daily Log	Records problems and concerns to be handled informally by the Project Manager
End Project Report	Confirms handover of the project's products to the Project Board and assesses project performance against the **PID**
End Stage Report	Provides information about project performance and status for the stage to the Project Board
Exception Report	Describes an exception situation, its impact, options, and Project Manager recommendations to the Project Board
Highlight Report	Reports stage progress and status to the Project Board on a regularly scheduled basis
Issue Register	Captures and maintains information on all project issues that are being managed formally
Issue Report	Describes, assesses the impact and makes recommendations for issues that are being formally handled
Lessons Log	Provides an informal repository for lessons learned that apply to the current project and lessons from previous projects
Lessons Report	Documents lessons learned from the current project that can be applied to future projects
Plan – Project, Stage and Team	Specifies the 'what, when, how and by whom' required to achieve an objective at a project, stage, or team level
Product Description	Describes the purpose, composition, derivation and quality criteria for a product
Product Status Account	Reports product status by identifier or the part of the project where they were developed
Project Brief	States the purpose, cost, time and performance requirements and constraints for a project

Project Initiation Document	Logical set of documents bringing together key information to start and to manage and control a project
Project Product Description	Defines project scope and requirements, customer quality expectation and acceptance criteria
Quality Management Strategy	Defines quality techniques, standards and responsibilities to be applied during a project
Quality Register	Contains summary details of all planned and completed quality activities for the project
Risk Management Strategy	Describes goals, procedures, roles and responsibilities, tolerance, tools and techniques for applying risk management
Risk Register	Records identified project risks, their status and history
Work Package	Contains information for creating one or more products, describing the products, the work and any constraints

Prince 2 Process Overview – High Level

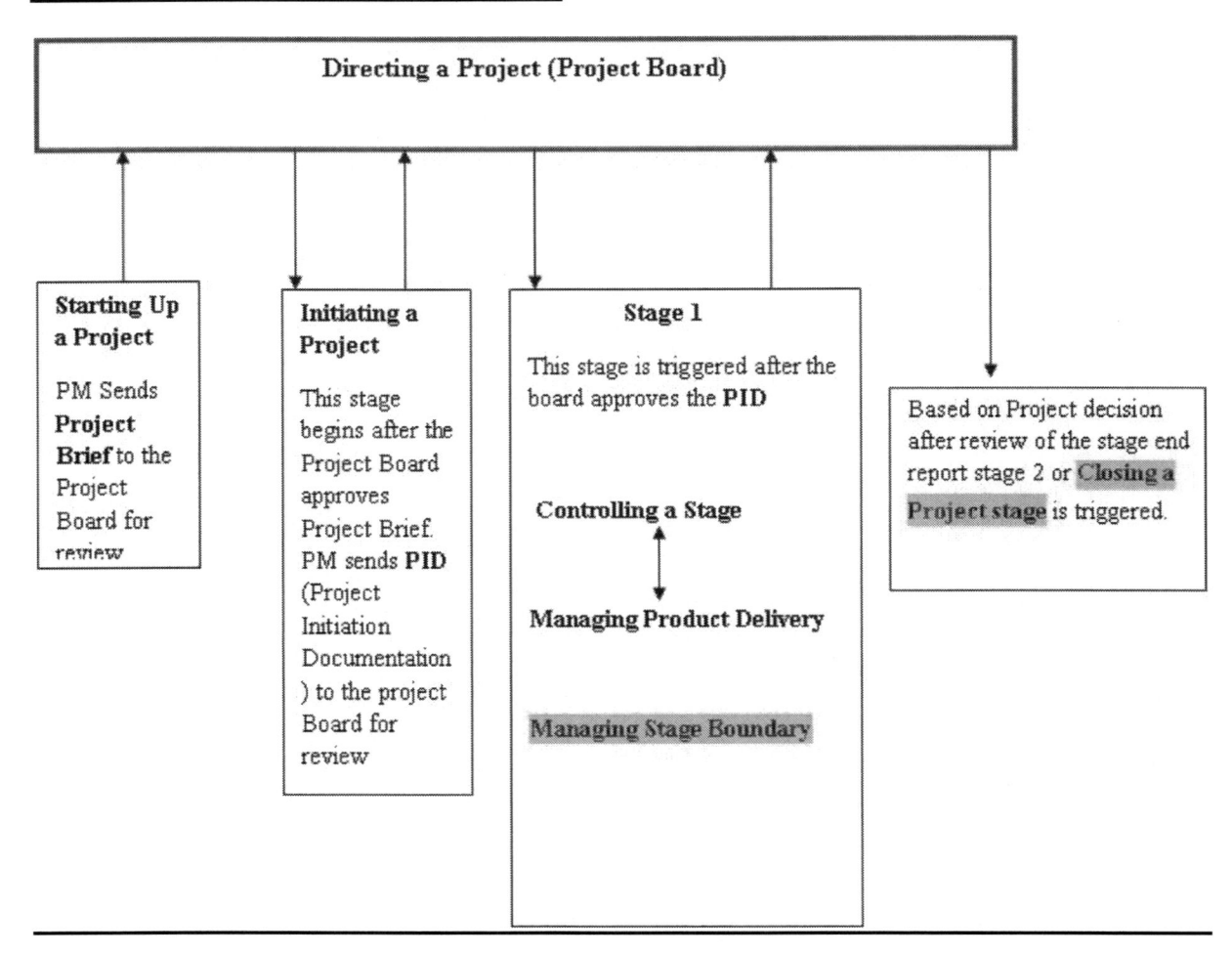

Directing a Project (Project Board)

Starting Up a Project

PM Sends **Project Brief** to the Project Board for review

Initiating a Project

This stage begins after the Project Board approves Project Brief. PM sends **PID** (Project Initiation Documentation) to the project Board for review

Stage 1

This stage is triggered after the board approves the **PID**

Controlling a Stage

↕

Managing Product Delivery

Managing Stage Boundary

Based on Project decision after review of the stage end report stage 2 or **Closing a Project stage** is triggered.

Prince 2 Process Overview – Detailed

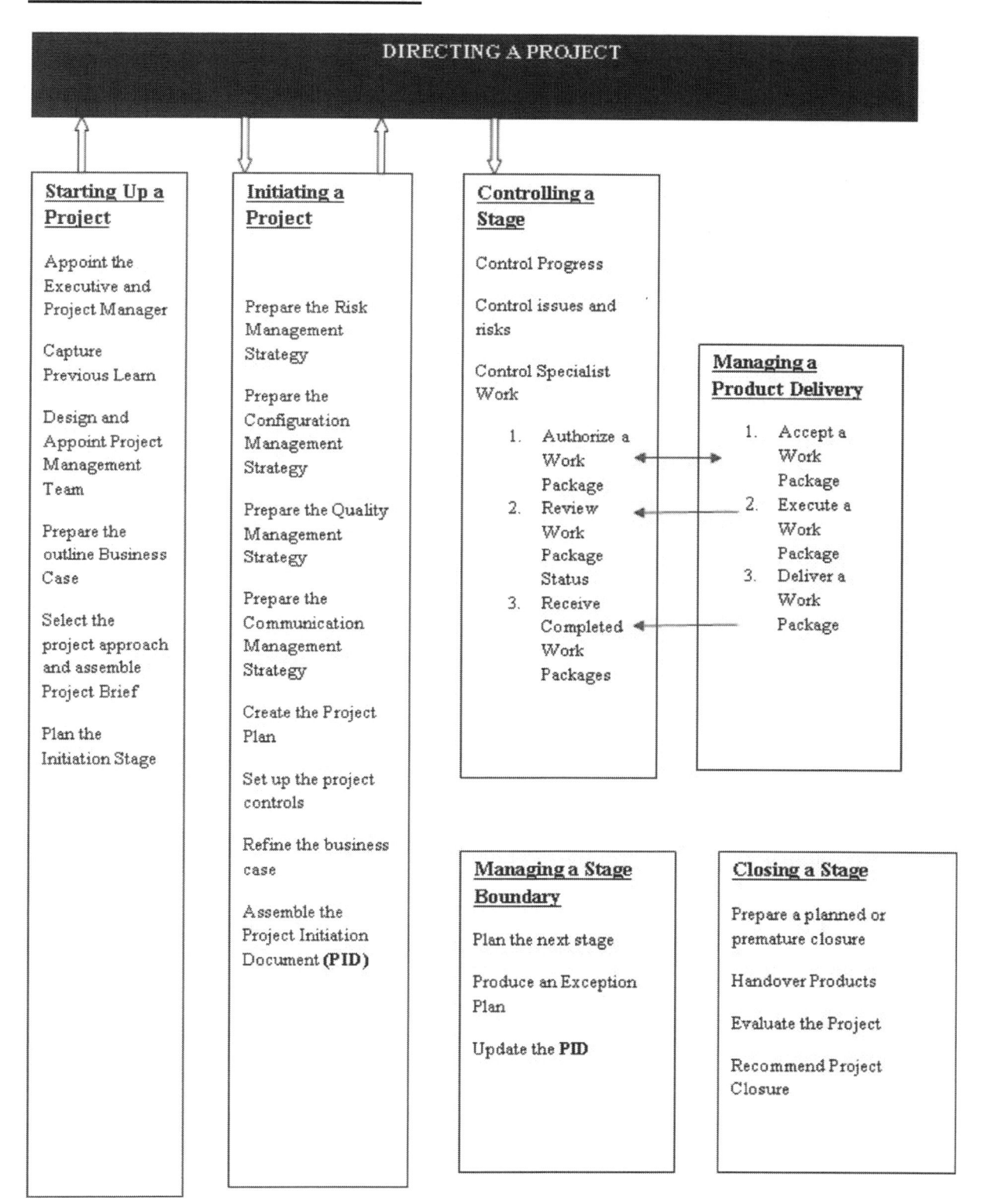

DIRECTING A PROJECT

Starting Up a Project

Appoint the Executive and Project Manager

Capture Previous Learn

Design and Appoint Project Management Team

Prepare the outline Business Case

Select the project approach and assemble Project Brief

Plan the Initiation Stage

Initiating a Project

Prepare the Risk Management Strategy

Prepare the Configuration Management Strategy

Prepare the Quality Management Strategy

Prepare the Communication Management Strategy

Create the Project Plan

Set up the project controls

Refine the business case

Assemble the Project Initiation Document **(PID)**

Controlling a Stage

Control Progress

Control issues and risks

Control Specialist Work

1. Authorize a Work Package
2. Review Work Package Status
3. Receive Completed Work Packages

Managing a Product Delivery

1. Accept a Work Package
2. Execute a Work Package
3. Deliver a Work Package

Managing a Stage Boundary

Plan the next stage

Produce an Exception Plan

Update the **PID**

Closing a Stage

Prepare a planned or premature closure

Handover Products

Evaluate the Project

Recommend Project Closure

Sample Paper -1

The Foundation Examination

Multiple Choice 1-hour paper Instructions

1. All 75 questions should be attempted.
2. 5 of the 75 questions are under trial and will not contribute to your Overall score. There is no indication of which questions are under trial.
3. All answers are to be marked on the answer sheet provided.
4. Please use a pencil and NOT ink to mark your answers on the answer sheet provided. There is only one correct answer per question.
5. You have 1 hour for this paper.
6. You must get 35 or more correct to pass.

Candidate Number: ....……

1. Which is a purpose of a Risk Register?

a) Capture risks that may occur during the project
b) Record how risk management activities will be undertaken on the project
c) Record the risk tolerance for the project
d) Capture issues which are impacting on the delivery of the project objectives

2. Which aspect of project performance must be managed to ensure the project's products are fit for purpose?

a. Benefits
b. Quality
c. Risk
d. Scope

3. What process provides the information required to decide whether to authorize the delivery of a project?

a. Directing a Project
b. Initiating a Project
c. Managing Product Delivery
d. Starting up a Project

4. Identify the missing words in the following sentence. A purpose of the Managing a Stage Boundary process is to produce [?] if the Project Board request the current stage is replanned following a tolerance deviation.

a. an Exception Report
b. an Exception Plan
c. a Stage Plan for the next stage
d. an updated Stage Plan

5. What product forms the 'contract' between the Project Board and the Project Manager?

a. Project Brief

b. Project Initiation Documentation
c. Project mandate
d. Project Plan

6. What is the collective name for individuals or groups who may be affected by a project?

a. Customers
b. Project Support
c. Stakeholders
d. Team members

7. What product identifies the management stages and other major control points in a project?

a. Business Case
b. Project Plan
c. Work Package
d. Project Brief

8. Which is NOT a purpose of a Benefits Review Plan?

a. Define the period over which the cost-benefit analysis will be based
b. Support a review of the performance of the project's products in operational use
c. Define the scope, timing and ownership of the benefit reviews required
d. Describe how to measure and confirm benefits after the project is closed

9. Which is a purpose of quality planning?

a. Define the structure of the project management team
b. Detail the acceptance criteria, in order for the Project Board to agree the level of quality expected of the project's product
c. Document approval records for those project products that have met their quality criteria
d. Produce the Project Plan with resource and schedule information

10. Which should be funded by a change budget?

a. Increase in agreed scope
b. Initiation stage
c. Change Authority
d. Handover activities

11. Which regular report provides the Project Board with a summary of stage status?

a. Communication Management Strategy
b. Project Brief
c. Highlight Report
d. Checkpoint Report

12. Which product records any project outcomes perceived as negative by stakeholders?

a. Business Case
b. Project Plan
c. Communication Management Strategy
d. Project Product Description

13. Identify the missing words in the following sentence. The Team Manager should check the [?] for any interfaces that must be maintained while developing products.

a. Project Product Description
b. Project Plan
c. Checkpoint Report
d. Work Package

14. Which is an objective of the Controlling a Stage process?

a. Prepare a Stage Plan for the next stage
b. Obtain approvals for completed products
c. Prevent 'scope creep' by monitoring products for uncontrolled change
d. Make provision to address all open issues and risks, with follow-on action recommendations

15. Which is a task of product-based planning?

a. Identify activities and dependencies
b. Write the Project Product Description
c. Prepare the Work Packages
d. Produce the Product Status Account

16. What process provides progress information on a team's work to the Project Manager?

a. Controlling a Stage
b. Directing a Project
c. Managing a Stage Boundary
d. Managing Product Delivery

17. Which is the purpose of the Change theme?

a. Prevent change to baselined products
b. Identify, assess and control any potential and approved changes to baselined products
c. Establish mechanisms to monitor and compare actual achievements against those planned
d. Assess and control uncertainty

18. What is used to identify any organization or interested party who needs to be informed of project closure?

a. Configuration Management Strategy
b. Project management team structure
c. Communication Management Strategy
d. Project Brief

19. Which is a purpose of the Risk theme?

a. Establish a procedure to ensure every change is agreed by the relevant authority before it takes place
b. Establish a cost-effective procedure to identify, assess and control uncertainty
c. Establish mechanisms to control any unacceptable deviations from plan
d. Establish mechanisms to manage risks at the corporate or programme level of an organization

20. Which activity does NOT have to take place before the initiation of a project is authorized?

a. Appoint at least the Executive
b. Define the quality techniques to be applied during a project
c. Prepare an outline Business Case
d. Assemble a Project Brief

21. Which is shown in a product breakdown structure?

a. Management stages, major products and control points
b. In which order the products should be created
c. The major products that are to be developed in a plan
d. What resources are required to develop the products

22. Which is NOT a purpose of an Issue Report?

a. Define the consequences of implementing a change to a product
b. Provide a channel for the Project Manager to seek formal advice from the Project Board
c. Notify the Project Manager of a Work Package forecast deviation, a problem or concern
d. Ensure that all concessions are formally documented for audit purposes

23. Which is a purpose of the Quality theme?

a. Establish the mechanisms to judge whether a project is desirable and achievable
b. Look for ways to improve the effectiveness of the management of the project
c. Control uncertainty to improve the ability of the project to succeed
d. Establish mechanisms to control any unacceptable deviation

24. Which characteristic distinguishes a project from regular business operations?

a. Produces benefits
b. Introduces business change
c. Manages stakeholders
d. Incurs cost

25. Which is a purpose of the Controlling a Stage process?

   a. Assign work to be done and take corrective action to ensure that the stage remains within tolerance
   b. Provide a fixed reference point at which acceptance for the project product is confirmed
   c. Enable the Project Board to be provided with sufficient information to authorize the next stage
   d. Enable the organization to understand the work that needs to be done to deliver the project's products

26. Which is an objective of the Managing a Stage Boundary process?

   a. Ensure that work to be allocated to teams is authorized and agreed
   b. When in exception, prepare an Exception Plan as directed by the Project Board
   c. Define how and when all the project's products will be delivered and at what cost
   d. Control the delivery of the project's products

27. Which is a benefit of using PRINCE2?

   a. Provides a defined structure of accountability, delegation, authority and communication
   b. Includes techniques for critical path analysis and earned value analysis
   c. Enables a Project Manager to be accountable for the success of a project
   d. Prevents any changes once the scope of a project has been agreed

28. Which does the Executive need to ensure is in place before the project is initiated?

   a. All Work Packages are authorized
   b. An understanding of how the project will contribute to corporate objectives
   c. The Project Plan has been approved
   d. The Project Initiation Documentation is complete

29. Why would the Project Manager escalate an issue to the Project Board?

   a. The Project Board is responsible for determining the priority of all issues
   b. Direction is required on the best response for preventing the issue from occurring
   c. The issue is forecast to cause a deviation beyond stage tolerance and advice is required

d. Escalating issues is a means of providing the Project Board with a regular update on their status

30. Which is a typical core activity within a configuration management procedure?

a. Quality assurance
b. Risk management
c. Verification and audit
d. Progress reporting

31. Identify the missing word in the following sentence. The guiding obligations and good practices which determine whether the project is genuinely being managed using PRINCE2 form the [?] of the method.

a. Principles
b. Themes
c. Processes
d. Techniques

32. Which is a purpose of the Plans theme?

a. Define the means by which products will be verified as fit for purpose
b. Establish the project's structure of accountability
c. Assess and control uncertainty
d. Understand whether the targets are achievable

33. When considering risks, which describes an opportunity in a project?

a. An uncertain event that could have a negative impact on objectives
b. An uncertain event that could have a favorable impact on objectives
c. An event that has occurred resulting in a negative impact on objectives
d. An event that has occurred resulting in a favorable impact on objectives

34. Which of the following describes a use of a Configuration Item Record?

a. To record how changes to a product will be controlled
b. To provide information on the approval procedure for the Work Package
c. To record the history of a product
d. To pass responsibility for the delivery of a product to a Team Manager

35 Which of the following is a type of issue?

1. Problem/concern
2. Request for change
3. External product
4. Off-specification

a. 1, 2, 3
b. 1, 2, 4
c. 1, 3, 4
d. 2, 3, 4

36 Which is a Product Description used for?

a. To define any inherent risks in a product
b. To record the results of any quality checks carried out on a product
c. To define the quality criteria for a product
d. To record acceptance of a product following its quality check(s)

37 Who establishes and maintains the corporate organization's quality management system?

a. Project Assurance
b. Project Support
c. Quality assurance
d. Change Authority

38 Which role is responsible for the management of a risk assigned to it?

a. Project Support
b. Risk owner
c. Risk actionee
d. Project Assurance

39 Who should use the information in a Lessons Report to refine, change and improve the standards within a quality management system?

a. Corporate group
Project Board
b. Project Assurance
c. Executive

40 Which of the following are PRINCE2 integrated elements?

1. Activities
2. Principles
3. Processes
4. Themes

a) 1, 2, 3
b) 1, 2, 4
c) 1, 3, 4
d) 2, 3, 4

41 Who is the key project decision-maker in the project management team?

a) Corporate management
b) Executive
c) Change Authority
d) Project Manager

42 Which theme provides the controls to escalate any forecast beyond tolerance to the next management level?

a) Business Case
b) Plans
c) Progress
d) Quality

43 If Work Package tolerance is forecast to be exceeded, to whom should the Team Manager Report?

a) Corporate management
b) Project Board
c) Project Assurance
d) Project Manager

44 Which is an objective of the Directing a Project process?

a. Create and authorize the project mandate
b. Provide management control and direction
c. Control the day-to-day running of the project
d. Provide accurate progress information to the Project Manager

45 What is defined as a temporary organization that is created for the purpose of delivering one or more business products?

a) Corporate or programme management
b) A project
c) A product breakdown structure
d) A user group

46 What theme provides the justification for the project?

a) Quality
b) Plans
c) Progress
d) Business Case

47 Which is a difference between management and technical stages?

a) Management stages require planning and technical stages do not
b) Technical stages can overlap and management stages cannot
c) Management stages deliver products and technical stages do not
d) Technical stages require resources and management stages do not

48 Which theme addresses the need to have a strategy for communicating with stakeholders?

a. Quality
b. Organization
c. Plans
d. Progress

49 In which product would you find quality tolerance defined?

a) Product Description
b) Project Plan
c) Quality Register
d) Configuration Item Record

50 Which is a purpose of the Closing a Project process?

a) Provide a fixed point at which acceptance for the project product is confirmed
b) Receive the completed Work Packages for the work performed in the final stage
c) Identify who will perform the activities to close a project
d) Recognize that the objectives set out in the original Project Brief have been achieved

51 Which is an objective of the Closing a Project process?

a) Review and approve the plan for project closure
b) Review the performance of the project against its baseline
c) Perform any post-project reviews
d) Create a Benefits Review Plan

52 Which is NOT a purpose of the Directing a Project process?

a. Enable the Project Board to be accountable for a project's success by making key decisions
b. Enable the Project Board to authorize Work Packages
c. Enable the Project Board to delegate day-to-day management of a project to its Project Manager

d. Enable the Project Board to exercise overall control of a project

53 Identify the missing words in the following sentence. During the Initiating a Project process the [?] before a project is authorized.

a. Minimum necessary is done to decide if a project is worthwhile
b. aim is to establish sound foundations to achieve a successful project
c. Project Brief is assembled and approved
d. project approach appropriate for delivering a project is selected

54 Which is created during the Starting up a Project process?

a) Project mandate
b) Project management team role descriptions
c) Communication Management Strategy
d) Quality Register

55 Which describes risk impact?

a) Timeframe within which the risk might occur
b) The trigger that occurred giving rise to the risk
c) The effect of the risk on the delivery of project objectives
d) How likely the risk is to occur in a given project situation

56 Which of the following are true statements for a Project Plan?

1. Used by the Project Board to monitor project progress
2. Identifies the major control points
3. Used as the basis for day-to-day control by the Project Manager
4. Should align to the corporate or programme management's plan

a) 1, 2, 3
b) 1, 2, 4
c) 1, 3, 4
d) 2, 3, 4

57 Which is a responsibility of Project Support?

a. Approving or rejecting issues
b. Setting of stage tolerances
c. Assessing whether quality control procedures are used correctly
d. Controlling and protecting the project's products

58 Identify the missing word(s) in the following sentence.

Following initiation, the Controlling a Stage process is used to manage and control each [?] of a project.

a) technical stage
b) benefit
c) management stage
d) Team Plan

59 If, during the Managing a Stage Boundary process, external factors are identified that may affect the business justification for a project, which product should be updated?

a) Business Case
b) Project Brief
c) End Project Report
d) Highlight Report

60 Which is a purpose of a Lessons Log?

a) Note lessons raised in the Checkpoint Report
b) Record that corrective action is being taken
c) Escalate lessons to the Project Board
d) Raise improvements with Project Assurance

61 Which is a true statement about acceptance criteria?

a) Acceptance criteria are used to produce the customer's quality expectations
b) Acceptance criteria are less specific and precise than customer's quality expectations
c) Once agreed, acceptance criteria CANNOT be changed

d) Acceptance criteria should be agreed between the customer and the supplier

62 What process is used by the Project Board to respond to an Exception Report?

a) Controlling a Stage
b) Managing a Stage Boundary
c) Managing Product Delivery
d) Directing a Project

63 When considering how long the project stages should be, which might be a reason for one stage to be longer than others?

a. A substantial amount of the project budget is to be spent
b. More human resources are required than in other stages
c. The risk is lower
d. No changes to the project management team are envisaged

64 Which risk response type is NOT recommended to respond to an opportunity?

a. Accept
b. Exploit
c. Share
d. Reject

65 Which is a purpose of a Business Case?

a. State and justify the business rationale for undertaking a project
b. Forecast who will be responsible for measurement of the expected benefits
c. Define the project approach
d. Describe what a project must deliver to gain customer acceptance

66 Identify the missing words in the following sentence. The [?] is one of the levels of plan recommended by PRINCE2.

a. Benefits Review Plan
b. Exception Plan
c. Product Status Account
d. Stage Plan

67 Which role is part of the project management team?

a. Change Authority
b. Quality assurance
c. Stakeholder
d. Corporate or programme management

68 Which describes the 'Identify Risks' step within the recommended risk management procedure?

a. Identify responses to risks documented in the Business Case
b. Gather information about the project environment and objectives
c. Identify the roles to be involved in risk management activities
d. Identify uncertainties that may impact on the delivery of the project objectives

69 When are project closure activities planned?

a. During the initiation stage
b. When the Stage Plan for the final management stage is produced
c. As the first activity in the Closing a Project process
d. In the last Work Package allocated to a Team Manager

70 Which is a purpose of a Lessons Report?

a. Improve the project management method for future projects
b. Detail open issues and risks that need to be managed after the project has closed
c. Compare the actual performance of the final stage against its plan
d. Provide a summary of the benefits realized during the project

71 Which is a purpose of the Managing Product Delivery process?

a. Enable the Senior Supplier to be provided with sufficient information by the Project Manager so that they can review the success of the current Work Package
b. Provide a controlled link between the Project Manager and the Team Manager(s)
c. Enable the Project Board to request updates to the current Team Plan
d. Establish solid foundations for the project

72 Which may be funded from a risk budget?

a. Corrections due to off-specifications
b. Impact analysis of requests for change
c. Implementation of a fallback plan
d. Preparation of the Risk Management Strategy

73 Which is a purpose of a Project Brief?

a. Acts as a base document against which the Project Board can assess progress, issues and ongoing viability questions
b. Provides a sound basis for project initiation
c. Defines how and when a measurement of the achievement of the project's benefits can be made
d. Provides a description of the means and frequency of communication

74 Which is NOT a recommended quality review team role?

a. Administrator
b. Chair
c. Producer
d. Reviewer

75 What is described as an organization's unique attitude towards risk taking

a) Risk appetite
b) Risk management
c) Risk evaluation
d) Risk tolerance

<u>Note - Answer of the questions (Sample Paper 1) are Mark in Bold</u>

1. Which is a purpose of a Risk Register?

   a) Capture risks that may occur during the project
   b) Record how risk management activities will be undertaken on the project
   c) Record the risk tolerance for the project
   d) Capture issues which are impacting on the delivery of the project objectives

2. Which aspect of project performance must be managed to ensure the project's products are fit for purpose?

   a. Benefits
   b. Quality
   c. Risk
   d. Scope

3. What process provides the information required to decide whether to authorize the delivery of a project?

   a. Directing a Project
   b. Initiating a Project
   c. Managing Product Delivery
   d. Starting up a Project

4. Identify the missing words in the following sentence. A purpose of the Managing a Stage Boundary process is to produce [?] if the Project Board request the current stage is replanned following a tolerance deviation.

   a. an Exception Report
   b. an Exception Plan
   c. a Stage Plan for the next stage
   d. an updated Stage Plan

5. What product forms the 'contract' between the Project Board and the Project Manager?

a. Project Brief
b. Project Initiation Documentation
c. Project mandate
d. Project Plan

6. What is the collective name for individuals or groups who may be affected by a project?

a. Customers
b. Project Support
c. Stakeholders
d. Team members

7. What product identifies the management stages and other major control points in a project?

a. Business Case
b. Project Plan
c. Work Package
d. Project Brief

8. Which is **NOT** a purpose of a Benefits Review Plan?

a. Define the period over which the cost-benefit analysis will be based
b. Support a review of the performance of the project's products in operational use
c. Define the scope, timing and ownership of the benefit reviews required
d. Describe how to measure and confirm benefits after the project is closed

9. Which is a purpose of quality planning?

a. Define the structure of the project management team
b. Detail the acceptance criteria, in order for the Project Board to agree the level of quality expected of the project's product

c. Document approval records for those project products that have met their quality criteria
d. Produce the Project Plan with resource and schedule information

10. Which should be funded by a change budget?

a. Increase in agreed scope
b. Initiation stage
c. Change Authority
d. Handover activities

11. Which regular report provides the Project Board with a summary of stage status?

a. Communication Management Strategy
b. Project Brief
c. Highlight Report
d. Checkpoint Report

12. Which product records any project outcomes perceived as negative by stakeholders?

a. Business Case
b. Project Plan
c. Communication Management Strategy
d. Project Product Description

13. Identify the missing words in the following sentence. The Team Manager should check the [?] for any interfaces that must be maintained while developing products.

a. Project Product Description
b. Project Plan
c. Checkpoint Report
d. Work Package

14. Which is an objective of the Controlling a Stage process?

e. Prepare a Stage Plan for the next stage
f. Obtain approvals for completed products
a. Prevent 'scope creep' by monitoring products for uncontrolled change

b. **Make provision to address all open issues and risks, with follow-on action recommendations**

15. Which is a task of product-based planning?

a. Identify activities and dependencies
b. **Write the Project Product Description**
c. Prepare the Work Packages
d. Produce the Product Status Account

16. What process provides progress information on a team's work to the Project Manager?

a. Controlling a Stage
b. Directing a Project
c. Managing a Stage Boundary
d. **Managing Product Delivery**

17. Which is the purpose of the Change theme?

a. Prevent change to baselined products
b. **Identify, assess and control any potential and approved changes to baselined products**
c. Establish mechanisms to monitor and compare actual achievements against those planned
d. Assess and control uncertainty

18. What is used to identify any organization or interested party who needs to be informed of project closure?

a. Configuration Management Strategy
b. Project management team structure
c. **Communication Management Strategy**
d. Project Brief

19. Which is a purpose of the Risk theme?

a. Establish a procedure to ensure every change is agreed by the relevant authority before it takes place
b. **Establish a cost-effective procedure to identify, assess and control uncertainty**
c. Establish mechanisms to control any unacceptable deviations from plan
d. Establish mechanisms to manage risks at the corporate or programme level of an organization

20. Which activity does **NOT** have to take place before the initiation of a project is authorized?

a. Appoint at least the Executive
b. **Define the quality techniques to be applied during a project**
c. Prepare an outline Business Case
d. Assemble a Project Brief

21. Which is shown in a product breakdown structure?

a. Management stages, major products and control points
b. In which order the products should be created
c. **The major products that are to be developed in a plan**
d. What resources are required to develop the products

22. Which is NOT a purpose of an Issue Report?

a. Define the consequences of implementing a change to a product
b. Provide a channel for the Project Manager to seek formal advice from the Project Board
c. Notify the Project Manager of a Work Package forecast deviation, a problem or concern
d. **Ensure that all concessions are formally documented for audit purposes**

23. Which is a purpose of the Quality theme?

a. Establish the mechanisms to judge whether a project is desirable and achievable
b. Look for ways to improve the effectiveness of the management of the project
c. **Control uncertainty to improve the ability of the project to succeed**
d. Establish mechanisms to control any unacceptable deviation

24. Which characteristic distinguishes a project from regular business operations?

a. Produces benefits
b. **Introduces business change**
c. Manages stakeholders
d. Incurs cost

25. Which is a purpose of the Controlling a Stage process?

a. **Assign work to be done and take corrective action to ensure that the stage remains within tolerance**
b. Provide a fixed reference point at which acceptance for the project product is confirmed
c. Enable the Project Board to be provided with sufficient information to authorize the next stage
d. Enable the organization to understand the work that needs to be done to deliver the project's products

26. Which is an objective of the Managing a Stage Boundary process?

a. Ensure that work to be allocated to teams is authorized and agreed
b. **When in exception, prepare an Exception Plan as directed by the Project Board**
c. Define how and when all the project's products will be delivered and at what cost
d. Control the delivery of the project's products

27. Which is a benefit of using PRINCE2?

a. **Provides a defined structure of accountability, delegation, authority and communication**
b. Includes techniques for critical path analysis and earned value analysis
a. Enables a Project Manager to be accountable for the success of a project
b. Prevents any changes once the scope of a project has been agreed

28. Which does the Executive need to ensure is in place before the project is initiated?

a. All Work Packages are authorized

b. **An understanding of how the project will contribute to corporate objectives**
   c. The Project Plan has been approved
   d. The Project Initiation Documentation is complete

29. Why would the Project Manager escalate an issue to the Project Board?

   a. The Project Board is responsible for determining the priority of all issues
   b. Direction is required on the best response for preventing the issue from occurring
   c. **The issue is forecast to cause a deviation beyond stage tolerance and advice is required**
   d. Escalating issues is a means of providing the Project Board with a regular update on their status

30. Which is a typical core activity within a configuration management procedure?

   a. Quality assurance
   b. Risk management
   c. **Verification and audit**
   d. Progress reporting

31. Identify the missing word in the following sentence. The guiding obligations and good practices which determine whether the project is genuinely being managed using PRINCE2 form the [?] of the method.

   a. **Principles**
   b. Themes
   c. Processes
   d. Techniques

32. Which is a purpose of the Plans theme?

   a. **Define the means by which products will be verified as fit for purpose**
   b. Establish the project's structure of accountability
   c. Assess and control uncertainty
   d. Understand whether the targets are achievable

33. When considering risks, which describes an opportunity in a project?

a. An uncertain event that could have a negative impact on objectives
b. An uncertain event that could have a favorable impact on objectives
c. An event that has occurred resulting in a negative impact on objectives
d. An event that has occurred resulting in a favorable impact on objectives

34. Which of the following describes a use of a Configuration Item Record?

a. To record how changes to a product will be controlled
b. To provide information on the approval procedure for the Work Package
c. To record the history of a product
d. To pass responsibility for the delivery of a product to a Team Manager

35 Which of the following is a type of issue?

1. Problem/concern
2. Request for change
3. External product
4. Off-specification

a. 1, 2, 3
b. 1, 2, 4
c. 1, 3, 4
d. 2, 3, 4

36 Which is a Product Description used for?

e. To define any inherent risks in a product
a. To record the results of any quality checks carried out on a product
b. To define the quality criteria for a product
c. To record acceptance of a product following its quality check(s)

37 Who establishes and maintains the corporate organization's quality management system?

a. Project Assurance
b. Project Support
c. Quality assurance
d. Change Authority

38 Which role is responsible for the management of a risk assigned to it?

e. Project Support
a. Risk owner

b. Risk actionee
c. Project Assurance

39 Who should use the information in a Lessons Report to refine, change and improve the standards within a quality management system?

a. **Corporate group**
b. Project Board
c. Project Assurance
d. Executive

40 Which of the following are PRINCE2 integrated elements?

1. Activities
2. Principles
3. Processes
4. Themes

a) 1, 2, 3
b) 1, 2, 4
c) 1, 3, 4
d) 2, 3, 4

41 Who is the key project decision-maker in the project management team?

a) Corporate management
b) Executive
c) Change Authority
d) Project Manager

42 Which theme provides the controls to escalate any forecast beyond tolerance to the next management level?

a) Business Case
b) Plans
c) Progress
d) Quality

43 If Work Package tolerance is forecast to be exceeded, to whom should the Team Manager Report?

a) Corporate management
b) Project Board
c) Project Assurance
d) Project Manager

44 Which is an objective of the Directing a Project process?

a. Create and authorize the project mandate
b. Provide management control and direction
c. Control the day-to-day running of the project
d. Provide accurate progress information to the Project Manager

45 What is defined as a temporary organization that is created for the purpose of delivering one or more business products?

a) Corporate or programme management
b) A project
c) A product breakdown structure
d) A user group

46 What theme provides the justification for the project?

a) Quality
b) Plans
c) Progress
d) Business Case

47 Which is a difference between management and technical stages?

a) Management stages require planning and technical stages do not
b) Technical stages can overlap and management stages cannot
c) Management stages deliver products and technical stages do not
d) Technical stages require resources and management stages do not

48 Which theme addresses the need to have a strategy for communicating with stakeholders?

a. Quality
b. Organization
c. Plans
d. Progress

49 In which product would you find quality tolerance defined?

a) Product Description
b) Project Plan
c) Quality Register
d) Configuration Item Record

50 Which is a purpose of the Closing a Project process?

a) Provide a fixed point at which acceptance for the project product is confirmed
b) Receive the completed Work Packages for the work performed in the final stage
c) Identify who will perform the activities to close a project
d) Recognize that the objectives set out in the original Project Brief have been achieved

51 Which is an objective of the Closing a Project process?

a) Review and approve the plan for project closure
b) Review the performance of the project against its baseline
c) Perform any post-project reviews
d) Create a Benefits Review Plan

52 Which is NOT a purpose of the Directing a Project process?

a. Enable the Project Board to be accountable for a project's success by making key decisions
b. Enable the Project Board to authorize Work Packages
c. Enable the Project Board to delegate day-to-day management of a project to its Project Manager
d. Enable the Project Board to exercise overall control of a project

53 Identify the missing words in the following sentence. During the Initiating a Project process the [?] before a project is authorized.

e. Minimum necessary is done to decide if a project is worthwhile
f. aim is to establish sound foundations to achieve a successful project
g. Project Brief is assembled and approved
h. project approach appropriate for delivering a project is selected

54 Which is created during the Starting up a Project process?

a) Project mandate
b) Project management team role descriptions
c) Communication Management Strategy
d) Quality Register

55 Which describes risk impact?

a) Timeframe within which the risk might occur
b) The trigger that occurred giving rise to the risk
c) The effect of the risk on the delivery of project objectives
d) How likely the risk is to occur in a given project situation

56 Which of the following are true statements for a Project Plan?

1. Used by the Project Board to monitor project progress
2. Identifies the major control points
3. Used as the basis for day-to-day control by the Project Manager
4. Should align to the corporate or programme management's plan

a) 1, 2, 3

b) 1, 2, 4
c) 1, 3, 4
d) 2, 3, 4

57 Which is a responsibility of Project Support?

a. Approving or rejecting issues
b. Setting of stage tolerances
c. Assessing whether quality control procedures are used correctly
d. Controlling and protecting the project's products

58 Identify the missing word(s) in the following sentence.

Following initiation, the Controlling a Stage process is used to manage and control each [?] of a project.

a) technical stage
b) benefit
c) management stage
d) Team Plan

59 If, during the Managing a Stage Boundary process, external factors are identified that may affect the business justification for a project, which product should be updated?

a) Business Case
b) Project Brief
c) End Project Report
d) Highlight Report

60 Which is a purpose of a Lessons Log?

a) Note lessons raised in the Checkpoint Report
b) Record that corrective action is being taken
c) Escalate lessons to the Project Board
d) Raise improvements with Project Assurance

61 Which is a true statement about acceptance criteria?

a) Acceptance criteria are used to produce the customer's quality expectations
b) Acceptance criteria are less specific and precise than customer's quality expectations
c) Once agreed, acceptance criteria CANNOT be changed
d) Acceptance criteria should be agreed between the customer and the supplier

62 What process is used by the Project Board to respond to an Exception Report?

a) Controlling a Stage
b) Managing a Stage Boundary
c) Managing Product Delivery
d) Directing a Project

63 When considering how long the project stages should be, which might be a reason for one stage to be longer than others?

a. A substantial amount of the project budget is to be spent
b. More human resources are required than in other stages
c. The risk is lower
d. No changes to the project management team are envisaged

64 Which risk response type is **NOT** recommended to respond to an opportunity?

a. Accept
b. Exploit
c. Share
d. Reject

65 Which is a purpose of a Business Case?

a. State and justify the business rationale for undertaking a project
b. Forecast who will be responsible for measurement of the expected benefits
c. Define the project approach
d. Describe what a project must deliver to gain customer acceptance

66 Identify the missing words in the following sentence. The [?] is one of the levels of plan recommended by PRINCE2.

a. Benefits Review Plan
b. Exception Plan
c. Product Status Account
d. Stage Plan

67 Which role is part of the project management team?

a. Change Authority
b. Quality assurance
c. Stakeholder
d. Corporate or programme management

68 Which describes the 'Identify Risks' step within the recommended risk management procedure?

a. Identify responses to risks documented in the Business Case
b. Gather information about the project environment and objectives
c. Identify the roles to be involved in risk management activities
d. Identify uncertainties that may impact on the delivery of the project objectives

69 When are project closure activities planned?

a. During the initiation stage
b. When the Stage Plan for the final management stage is produced
c. As the first activity in the Closing a Project process
d. In the last Work Package allocated to a Team Manager

70 Which is a purpose of a Lessons Report?

a. Improve the project management method for future projects
b. Detail open issues and risks that need to be managed after the project has closed
c. Compare the actual performance of the final stage against its plan
d. Provide a summary of the benefits realized during the project

71 Which is a purpose of the Managing Product Delivery process?

a. Enable the Senior Supplier to be provided with sufficient information by the Project Manager so that they can review the success of the current Work Package
b. Provide a controlled link between the Project Manager and the Team Manager(s)

c. Enable the Project Board to request updates to the current Team Plan
d. Establish solid foundations for the project

72 Which may be funded from a risk budget?

a. Corrections due to off-specifications
b. Impact analysis of requests for change
c. Implementation of a fallback plan
d. Preparation of the Risk Management Strategy

73 Which is a purpose of a Project Brief?

a. Acts as a base document against which the Project Board can assess progress, issues and ongoing viability questions
b. Provides a sound basis for project initiation
c. Defines how and when a measurement of the achievement of the project's benefits can be made
d. Provides a description of the means and frequency of communication

74 Which is **NOT** a recommended quality review team role?

a. Administrator
b. Chair
c. Producer
d. Reviewer

75 What is described as an organization's unique attitude towards risk taking

a) Risk appetite
b) Risk management
c) Risk evaluation
d) Risk tolerance

Sample Paper - 2

The Foundation Examination

Multiple Choice

1-hour paper

Instructions

1. All 75 questions should be attempted.

2. 5 of the 75 questions are under trial and will not contribute to your overall score. There is no indication of which questions are under trial.

3. All answers are to be marked on the answer sheet provided.

4. Please use a pencil and NOT ink to mark your answers on the answer sheet provided. There is only one correct answer per question.

5. You have 1 hour for this paper.

6. You must get 35 or more correct to pass.

Candidate Number: ……………………………….…

1. Which does NOT reflect the PRINCE2 principle of continued business justification?

    a. There must be a justifiable reason for starting a project
    b. The business justification drives decision making
    c. If a project is no longer forecast to deliver a financial benefit, it should be stopped.
    d. If a project can no longer be justified, it should be stopped

2. Identify the missing words in the following sentence. The Starting up a Project process is triggered when a [?] is available.

    a. project Business Case
    b. project mandate
    c. Stage Plan
    d. Work Package

3. What do acceptance criteria identify?

    a. The approach that will be used to prove whether the project's products have been completed
    b. A measureable improvement resulting from a project outcome
    c. The measureable definitions of the attributes for a set of products to be acceptable to key stakeholders
    d. The project controls set up during the process Initiating a Project

4. Which is a typical core activity within a configuration management procedure?

    a. Assessment
    b. Communication
    c. Quality control
    d. Status accounting

5. Which is a risk cause?

    a. The actions required to resolve a risk
    b. The impact that a risk would have on a project if it materializes
    c. The likelihood of a risk occurring
    d. The source of a risk

6. Which statement describes the responsibilities of a risk actionee?

    a. Identifying risks to the project that might occur in their department
    b. Owning and authorizing the use of the risk budget to fund risk responses
    c. Managing, monitoring and controlling of all aspects of an assigned risk
    d. Carrying out a risk response action to respond to a particular risk

7. Which is a purpose of the Initiating a Project process?

    a. Produce a Stage Plan for each stage of a multi-stage project
    b. Enable the Project Board to decide whether it is worthwhile to initiate a project
    c. Provide a fixed point at which acceptance for the project product is confirmed
    d. Enable an organization to understand the work that needs to be done to deliver the project's products

8. Identify the missing words in the following sentence. The Managing a Stage Boundary process should be executed [?] a management stage.

    a. when a Stage Plan has been prepared for
    b. at the beginning of
    c. when all the technical stages have been completed within
    d. at, or close to the end of,

9. During the Managing a Stage Boundary process, what is reviewed and updated to provide the information needed by the Project Board for assessing the continuing viability of the project?

    a. Benefits Review Plan
    b. Product Status Account
    c. Business Case
    d. Project Plan

10. What product provides details about the latest version numbers of a project's products?

    a. Project Product Description
    b. Product Status Account
    c. Project Plan
    d. Issue Register

11. Which characteristic distinguishes a project from regular business operations?

    a. Produces benefits
    b. Introduces business change
    c. Manages stakeholders
    d. Incurs cost

12. What is the PRINCE2 definition of a project?

    a. The mechanism used to monitor and compare actual achievements against those planned
    b. A temporary organization that is created for the purpose of delivering business products
    c. A sequence of activities to manage product creation
    d. Defined and agreed roles and responsibilities within an organization structure that engages the business, user and supplier stakeholder interests

13. Which two roles are linked by the Managing Product Delivery process?

    a. Corporate or programme management and Project Board
    b. Project Board and Project Manager
    c. Project Manager and Team Manager
    d. Team Manager and external supplier

14. Identify the missing word in the following sentence. A project's [?] is any of the project's specialist products.

    a. benefit
    b. dis-benefit
    c. outcome
    d. output

15. Which is a purpose of the Controlling a Stage process?

    a. Assign work to be done and take corrective action to ensure that the stage remains within tolerance
    b. Provide a fixed reference point at which acceptance for the project product is confirmed
    c. Enable the Project Board to be provided with sufficient information to authorize the next stage
    d. Enable the organization to understand the work that needs to be done to deliver the project's products

16. What product identifies the management stages and other major control points in a project?

    a. Business Case
    b. Project Plan
    c. Work Package
    d. Project Brief

17. Which of the following would be recorded in an Issue Register?

    1. Problems that require formal management
    2. Risks with high probability
    3. Suggested improvements to baselined products
    4. Requested additions to scope

    a. 1, 2, 3
    b. 1, 2, 4
    c. 1, 3, 4
    d. 2, 3, 4

18. Which of the following describe a purpose of the Benefits Review Plan?

    1. Identifies when measurement of the achievement of the project's benefits can be made
    2. Used during the Closing a Project process to define any post-project benefits reviews that are required
    3. Includes the activities required to find out how the products perform when in operational use
    4. Defines the justification for undertaking the project

    a. 1, 2, 3
    b. 1, 2, 4
    c. 1, 3, 4
    d. 2, 3, 4

19. In which product does a Project Manager define the time and cost tolerances for the work to be done by a Team Manager?

    a. Product Description
    b. Team Plan
    c. Work Package
    d. Stage Plan

20. Which is a purpose of an End Stage Report?

    a. Support the Project Board's decision on what action to take next
    b. Summarize how the project performed against the version of the Project Initiation Documentation used to authorize it
    c. Provide the detailed analysis of a deviation and offer options for the way to proceed
    d. Provide a plan for the next stage of the project

21. Which step in the issue and change control procedure evaluates options to respond to an Issue that is being managed formally?

    a. Capture
    b. Examine
    c. Propose
    d. Decide

22. What process is used by the Project Board to respond to an Exception Report?

    a. Controlling a Stage
    b. Managing a Stage Boundary
    c. Managing Product Delivery
    d. Directing a Project

23. Which action should be taken within the Closing a Project process to ensure benefits that still need to be realized are measured?

    a. Prevent closure of a project until all benefits are realized
    b. Update a Benefits Review Plan with the dates of post-project benefits reviews
    c. Create a follow-on action recommendation for each benefit yet to be measured
    d. Make the role of Project Manager responsible for the measurement of benefits once a project is closed

24. Which is a purpose of the Managing a Stage Boundary process?

    a. Provide the Project Board with sufficient information for approving the next stage
    b. Approve the next Stage Plan
    c. Review and close any risks and issues identified during the previous stage
    d. Control the link between the Project Manager and the Team Manager(s)

25. Which process covers the work done by external suppliers who may NOT be using PRINCE2?

    a. Closing a Project
    b. Managing a Stage Boundary
    c. Managing Product Delivery
    d. Directing a Project

26. Which role does NOT set tolerances?

    a. Corporate or programme management
    b. Project Board
    c. Change Authority
    d. Project Manager

27. What process provides progress information on a team's work to the Project Manager?

    a. Controlling a Stage
    b. Directing a Project
    c. Managing a Stage Boundary
    d. Managing Product Delivery

28. Which statement is true for project stakeholders?

    a. All stakeholders must be identified at the start of the project
    b. Stakeholders are NOT members of the Project Board
    c. All stakeholders are external to the corporate organization
    d. All three primary categories of stakeholder have their interests represented by the Project Board

29. Which product describes the roles and responsibilities for achieving the effective management of anticipated threats and opportunities in a project?

    a. Quality Management Strategy
    b. Risk Management Strategy
    c. Communication Management Strategy
    d. Configuration Management Strategy

30. Which is a purpose of a Project Brief?

    a. Enable the assembly of the project mandate
    b. Describe the reporting requirements of the various layers of management involved with the project
    c. Describe how changes to products will be controlled
    d. Provide a solid basis for the initiation of the project

31. What is the first task of product-based planning?

    a. Produce the Initiation Stage Plan
    b. Write the Project Product Description
    c. Identify dependencies
    d. Create the product breakdown structure

32. Which product is used by the Project Manager to authorize work?

    a. Team Plan
    b. Stage Plan
    c. Work Package
    d. Product Description

33. Which of the following are PRINCE2 principles?

    1. Continued business justification
    2. Defined roles and responsibilities
    3. Customer/supplier environment
    4. Learn from experience

    a. 1, 2, 3
    b. 1, 2, 4
    c. 1, 3, 4
    d. 2, 3, 4

34. Which is a purpose of quality planning?

    a. Define the structure of the project management team
    b. Detail the acceptance criteria, in order for the Project Board to agree the level of quality expected of the project's product
    c. Document approval records for those project products that have met their quality criteria
    d. Produce the Project Plan with resource and schedule information

35. Which is NOT a recommended quality review team role?

    a. Administrator
    b. Chair
    c. Producer
    d. Reviewer

36. Why is it crucial that the Project Product Description clearly defines acceptance methods?

    a. Enables Project Assurance to authorize quality activities
    b. Defines how all project products will be reviewed and approved
    c. Defines how it will be proven that the completed project product meets the customer's expectations
    d. Provides confirmation that all project products have met their quality criteria

37. Which is the Change Authority role permitted to authorize?

    a. Risks to the project
    b. Adjustments to the limits on the change budget
    c. Changes to stage tolerance
    d. Changes to the project that do not exceed a defined budget

38. Which aspect of project performance must be managed to avoid misunderstandings on what the project is to deliver?

    a. Timescale
    b. Scope
    c. Risk
    d. Costs

39. Which does the Change theme consider a prerequisite for effective issue and change control?

    a. Configuration management system
    b. Manage by exception
    c. Quality planning
    d. Information needs for stakeholders

40. What product is used to maintain a record of those who have an interest in the project and their information requirements?

    a. Project Plan
    b. Communication Management Strategy
    c. Project Brief
    d. Project Product Description

41. If Work Package tolerance is forecast to be exceeded, to whom should the Team Manager report?

    a. Corporate management
    b. Project Board
    c. Project Assurance
    d. Project Manager

42. Which is NOT undertaken during the Initiating a Project process?

    a. Review why the project is needed
    b. Identify if the project is sufficiently aligned with corporate objectives
    c. Show how the outcome is to be achieved
    d. Appoint an Executive and Project Manager

43. Which describes risk appetite?

    a. An organization's unique attitude towards risk-taking
    b. The risks to the expected benefits
    c. A common set of risk categories, risk scales and evaluation techniques
    d. The budget set aside for potential changes to the scope of the project

44. Which is a type of issue?

    a. A lesson
    b. A request for change
    c. An Exception Report
    d. A risk with an estimated high impact

45. What product would enable the Project Manager to review how a Work Package is performing against its cost tolerance?

    a. Configuration Item Record
    b. Quality Register
    c. Highlight Report
    d. Checkpoint Report

46. Identify the missing word(s) in the following sentence. PRINCE2 recommends three levels of [?] to reflect the needs of the different levels of management involved in a project.

    a. Management strategies
    b. Plan
    c. Stakeholder interests
    d. Time-driven controls

47. Which is NOT a purpose of the Directing a Project process?

    a. Enable the Project Board to be accountable for a project's success by making key decisions
    b. Enable the Project Board to authorize Work Packages
    c. Enable the Project Board to delegate day-to-day management of a project to its Project Manager
    d. Enable the Project Board to exercise overall control of a project

48. Which theme defines the accountability for realization of the project's benefits?

    a. Plans
    b. Progress
    c. Organization
    d. Quality

49. Which role is part of the Project Board?

    a. Corporate or programme management
    b. Risk owner
    c. Project Manager
    d. Senior Supplier

50. Which risk response type is appropriate to respond to a threat?

    a. Exploit
    b. Enhance
    c. Reject
    d. Transfer

51. Which of the following is NOT identified in a Product Description?

    a. The quality specification to which a product must be produced
    b. The purpose a product must fulfill
    c. The skills required to undertake quality control of a product
    d. The time and cost tolerances for the creation of a product

52. Identify the missing words in the following sentence. At the end of a stage, the [?] should be used to check whether there is a requirement to send copies of the End Stage Report to external interested parties.

    a. Stage Plan
    b. Communication Management Strategy
    c. Follow-on action recommendations
    d. Quality Management Strategy

53. Which theme provides the controls to escalate any forecast beyond tolerance to the next management level?

    a. Business Case
    b. Plans
    c. Progress
    d. Quality

54. Which provides a single source of reference that may be used by people joining a project after it has been initiated so they can quickly and easily find out how the project is being managed?

    a. Project Brief
    b. Project Initiation Documentation
    c. Project mandate
    d. Project Product Description

55. During the Initiating a Project process, which product is updated to incorporate the estimated time and costs from the Project Plan?

    a. Project Product Description
    b. Business Case
    c. Project Brief
    d. Project mandate

56. Which is a purpose of the Risk theme?

    a. Establish a procedure to ensure every change is agreed by the relevant authority before it takes place
    b. Establish a cost-effective procedure to identify, assess and control uncertainty
    c. Establish mechanisms to control any unacceptable deviations from plan
    d. Establish mechanisms to manage risks at the corporate or programme level of an organization

57. Which is a benefit of using PRINCE2?

    a. Provides a defined structure of accountability, delegation, authority and communication
    b. Includes techniques for critical path analysis and earned value analysis
    c. Enables a Project Manager to be accountable for the success of a project
    d. Prevents any changes once the scope of a project has been agreed

58. Who carries out audits that are independent of the project?

    a. Quality assurance
    b. Project Assurance
    c. Project Support
    d. Project Manager

59. Which is a task of product-based planning?

    a. Design the plan
    b. Create the product flow diagram
    c. Analyze the risks
    d. Prepare the schedule

60. What theme establishes the mechanisms to judge whether a project is worthwhile investing in?

    a. Plans
    b. Business Case
    c. Risk
    d. Quality

61. If a project's benefit tolerance is forecast to be exceeded, to whom should this be escalated to for a decision?
    a. Senior User
    b. Executive
    c. Corporate/programme management
    d. Senior Supplier

62. Which does the Executive need to ensure is in place before the project is initiated?

    a. All Work Packages are authorized
    b. An understanding of how the project will contribute to corporate objectives
    c. The Project Plan has been approved
    d. The Project Initiation Documentation is complete

63. Which is a purpose of the Starting up a Project process?

    a. Provide information so a decision can be made as to whether a project is viable and worthwhile to initiate
    b. Define the means of communication between the project and corporate or programme management
    c. Define the project controls
    d. Record any identified risks in the Risk Register

64. Which is a purpose of the 'Plan' step within the recommended risk management procedure?

    a. Identify the roles and responsibilities for all risk management activities
    b. Prepare and agree the Risk Management Strategy with the Project Board
    c. Plan the Communication Management Strategy to keep stakeholders updated on the risk management activities
    d. Identify possible responses to be implemented to manage a risk should it occur

65. Which describes risk impact?

    a. Timeframe within which the risk might occur
    b. The trigger that occurred giving rise to the risk
    c. The effect of the risk on the delivery of project objectives
    d. How likely the risk is to occur in a given project situation

66. What process ensures focus on the delivery of a stage's products and avoids uncontrolled change?

    a. Directing a Project
    b. Managing a Stage Boundary
    c. Controlling a Stage
    d. Starting up a Project

67. Which is a difference between management and technical stages?

   a. Management stages require planning and technical stages do not
   b. Technical stages can overlap and management stages cannot
   c. Management stages deliver products and technical stages do not
   d. Technical stages require resources and management stages do not

68. Which should be funded from a change budget?

   a. The Starting up a Project process
   b. A fallback plan
   c. An agreed change to the scope of a project
   d. A change to a plan, within allocated tolerances, due to poor estimating

69. Which is a true statement about PRINCE2 event-driven controls?

   a. Event-driven controls take place at predefined periodic intervals
   b. Event-driven controls are produced at the frequency defined in a Work Package
   c. Event-driven controls are used for decision making
   d. Checkpoint Reports are event-driven controls

70. What theme estimates the cost of delivering the project?

   a. Business Case
   b. Change
   c. Plans
   d. Progress

71. What takes place during the Closing a Project process?

   a. The post-project benefits reviews are performed
   b. Ownership of the project's products is transferred to the customer
   c. An End Stage Report is prepared for the final stage
   d. The project closure notification is reviewed and approved

72. Which is an objective of the quality review technique?

   a. To provide confirmation that a product is complete and ready for approval
   b. To identify solutions to defects found during the quality review meeting
   c. To agree the quality criteria for the product under review
   d. To enable changes to be agreed and added to a baselined product

73. Which is an objective of the Directing a Project process?

    a. Review and approve a project mandate
    b. Ensure corporate or programme management has an interface to the project
    c. Define how risks, issues and changes will be managed
    d. Obtain approval for completed products

74. Which is a purpose of the Closing a Project process?

    a. Authorize the final stage of the project
    b. Confirm that all benefits defined in the Business Case have been achieved
    c. Recognize that objectives set out in the original Project Initiation Documentation have been achieved
    d. Delegate day-to-day management of the end of the project to the Project Manager

75. Identify the missing word in the following sentence. A risk consists of the [?] of a threat occurring and its impact.

    a. outcome
    b. probability
    c. dis-benefit
    d. proximity

Note - Answer of the questions (Sample Paper 2) are Mark in Bold

1. Which does **NOT** reflect the PRINCE2 principle of continued business justification?

    a. There must be a justifiable reason for starting a project
    b. The business justification drives decision making
    c. If a project is no longer forecast to deliver a financial benefit, it should be stopped.
    d. If a project can no longer be justified, it should be stopped

2. Identify the missing words in the following sentence. The Starting up a Project process is triggered when a [?] is available.

    a. project Business Case
    b. project mandate
    c. Stage Plan
    d. Work Package

3. What do acceptance criteria identify?

    a. The approach that will be used to prove whether the project's products have been completed
    b. A measureable improvement resulting from a project outcome
    c. The measureable definitions of the attributes for a set of products to be acceptable to key stakeholders
    d. The project controls set up during the process Initiating a Project

4. Which is a typical core activity within a configuration management procedure?

    a. Assessment
    b. Communication
    c. Quality control
    d. Status accounting

5. Which is a risk cause?

    a. The actions required to resolve a risk
    b. The impact that a risk would have on a project if it materializes
    c. The likelihood of a risk occurring
    d. The source of a risk

6. Which statement describes the responsibilities of a risk actionee?

    a. Identifying risks to the project that might occur in their department
    b. Owning and authorizing the use of the risk budget to fund risk responses
    c. Managing, monitoring and controlling of all aspects of an assigned risk
    d. Carrying out a risk response action to respond to a particular risk

7. Which is a purpose of the Initiating a Project process?

    a. Produce a Stage Plan for each stage of a multi-stage project
    b. Enable the Project Board to decide whether it is worthwhile to initiate a project
    c. Provide a fixed point at which acceptance for the project product is confirmed
    d. Enable an organization to understand the work that needs to be done to deliver the project's products

8. Identify the missing words in the following sentence. The Managing a Stage Boundary process should be executed [?] a management stage.

    a. when a Stage Plan has been prepared for
    b. at the beginning of
    c. when all the technical stages have been completed within
    d. at, or close to the end of,

9. During the Managing a Stage Boundary process, what is reviewed and updated to provide the information needed by the Project Board for assessing the continuing viability of the project?

    a. Benefits Review Plan
    b. Product Status Account
    c. Business Case
    d. Project Plan

10. What product provides details about the latest version numbers of a project's products?

    a. Project Product Description
    b. Product Status Account
    c. Project Plan
    d. Issue Register

11. Which characteristic distinguishes a project from regular business operations?

    a. Produces benefits
    b. Introduces business change
    c. Manages stakeholders
    d. Incurs cost

12. What is the PRINCE2 definition of a project?

    a. The mechanism used to monitor and compare actual achievements against those planned
    b. A temporary organization that is created for the purpose of delivering business products
    c. A sequence of activities to manage product creation
    d. Defined and agreed roles and responsibilities within an organization structure that engages the business, user and supplier stakeholder interests

13. Which two roles are linked by the Managing Product Delivery process?

    a. Corporate or programme management and Project Board
    b. Project Board and Project Manager
    c. Project Manager and Team Manager
    d. Team Manager and external supplier

14. Identify the missing word in the following sentence. A project's [?] is any of the project's specialist products.

    a. benefit
    b. dis-benefit
    c. outcome
    d. output

15. Which is a purpose of the Controlling a Stage process?

    a. Assign work to be done and take corrective action to ensure that the stage remains within tolerance
    b. Provide a fixed reference point at which acceptance for the project product is confirmed
    c. Enable the Project Board to be provided with sufficient information to authorize the next stage
    d. Enable the organization to understand the work that needs to be done to deliver the project's products

16. What product identifies the management stages and other major control points in a project?

    a. Business Case
    b. Project Plan
    c. Work Package
    d. Project Brief

17. Which of the following would be recorded in an Issue Register?

    1. Problems that require formal management
    2. Risks with high probability
    3. Suggested improvements to baselined products
    4. Requested additions to scope

    a. 1, 2, 3
    b. 1, 2, 4
    c. 1, 3, 4
    d. 2, 3, 4

18. Which of the following describe a purpose of the Benefits Review Plan?

    1. Identifies when measurement of the achievement of the project's benefits can be made
    2. Used during the Closing a Project process to define any post-project benefits reviews that are required
    3. Includes the activities required to find out how the products perform when in operational use
    4. Defines the justification for undertaking the project

    a. 1, 2, 3
    b. 1, 2, 4
    c. 1, 3, 4
    d. 2, 3, 4

19. In which product does a Project Manager define the time and cost tolerances for the work to be done by a Team Manager?

    e. Product Description
    a. Team Plan
    b. Work Package
    c. Stage Plan

141

20. Which is a purpose of an End Stage Report?

    a. **Support the Project Board's decision on what action to take next**
    b. Summarize how the project performed against the version of the Project Initiation Documentation used to authorize it
    c. Provide the detailed analysis of a deviation and offer options for the way to proceed
    d. Provide a plan for the next stage of the project

21. Which step in the issue and change control procedure evaluates options to respond to an Issue that is being managed formally?

    a. Capture
    b. Examine
    c. **Propose**
    d. Decide

22. What process is used by the Project Board to respond to an Exception Report?

    a. Controlling a Stage
    b. Managing a Stage Boundary
    c. Managing Product Delivery
    d. **Directing a Project**

23. Which action should be taken within the Closing a Project process to ensure benefits that still need to be realized are measured?

    a. Prevent closure of a project until all benefits are realized
    b. Update a Benefits Review Plan with the dates of post-project benefits reviews
    c. **Create a follow-on action recommendation for each benefit yet to be measured**
    d. Make the role of Project Manager responsible for the measurement of benefits once a project is closed

24. Which is a purpose of the Managing a Stage Boundary process?

    a. **Provide the Project Board with sufficient information for approving the next stage**
    b. Approve the next Stage Plan
    c. Review and close any risks and issues identified during the previous stage
    d. Control the link between the Project Manager and the Team Manager(s)

25. Which process covers the work done by external suppliers who may NOT be using PRINCE2?

    a. Closing a Project
    b. Managing a Stage Boundary
    c. **Managing Product Delivery**
    d. Directing a Project

26. Which role does NOT set tolerances?

    a. Corporate or programme management
    b. Project Board
    c. **Change Authority**
    d. Project Manager

27. What process provides progress information on a team's work to the Project Manager?

    a. Controlling a Stage
    b. Directing a Project
    c. Managing a Stage Boundary
    d. **Managing Product Delivery**

28. Which statement is true for project stakeholders?

    a. All stakeholders must be identified at the start of the project
    b. Stakeholders are NOT members of the Project Board
    c. All stakeholders are external to the corporate organization
    d. **All three primary categories of stakeholder have their interests represented by the Project Board**

29. Which product describes the roles and responsibilities for achieving the effective management of anticipated threats and opportunities in a project?

   a. Quality Management Strategy
   b. Risk Management Strategy
   c. Communication Management Strategy
   d. Configuration Management Strategy

30. Which is a purpose of a Project Brief?

   a. Enable the assembly of the project mandate
   b. Describe the reporting requirements of the various layers of management involved with the project
   c. Describe how changes to products will be controlled
   d. Provide a solid basis for the initiation of the project

31. What is the first task of product-based planning?

   a. Produce the Initiation Stage Plan
   b. Write the Project Product Description
   c. Identify dependencies
   d. Create the product breakdown structure

32. Which product is used by the Project Manager to authorize work?

   a. Team Plan
   b. Stage Plan
   c. Work Package
   d. Product Description

33. Which of the following are PRINCE2 principles?

   1. Continued business justification
   2. Defined roles and responsibilities
   3. Customer/supplier environment
   4. Learn from experience

   a. 1, 2, 3
   b. 1, 2, 4
   c. 1, 3, 4
   d. 2, 3, 4

34. Which is a purpose of quality planning?

    a. Define the structure of the project management team
    b. **Detail the acceptance criteria, in order for the Project Board to agree the level of quality expected of the project's product**
    c. Document approval records for those project products that have met their quality criteria
    d. Produce the Project Plan with resource and schedule information

35. Which is NOT a recommended quality review team role?

    a. Administrator
    b. Chair
    c. **Producer**
    d. Reviewer

36. Why is it crucial that the Project Product Description clearly defines acceptance methods?

    a. Enables Project Assurance to authorize quality activities
    b. Defines how all project products will be reviewed and approved
    c. **Defines how it will be proven that the completed project product meets the customer's expectations**
    d. Provides confirmation that all project products have met their quality criteria

37. Which is the Change Authority role permitted to authorize?

    a. Risks to the project
    b. Adjustments to the limits on the change budget
    c. **Changes to stage tolerance**
    d. Changes to the project that do not exceed a defined budget

38. Which aspect of project performance must be managed to avoid misunderstandings on what the project is to deliver?

    a. Timescale
    b. Scope
    c. Risk
    d. Costs

39. Which does the Change theme consider a prerequisite for effective issue and change control?

    a. Configuration management system
    b. Manage by exception
    c. Quality planning
    d. Information needs for stakeholders

40. What product is used to maintain a record of those who have an interest in the project and their information requirements?

    a. Project Plan
    b. Communication Management Strategy
    c. Project Brief
    d. Project Product Description

41. If Work Package tolerance is forecast to be exceeded, to whom should the Team Manager report?

    a. Corporate management
    b. Project Board
    c. Project Assurance
    d. Project Manager

42. Which is NOT undertaken during the Initiating a Project process?

    a. Review why the project is needed
    b. Identify if the project is sufficiently aligned with corporate objectives
    c. Show how the outcome is to be achieved
    d. Appoint an Executive and Project Manager

43. Which describes risk appetite?

    a. **An organization's unique attitude towards risk-taking**
    b. The risks to the expected benefits
    c. A common set of risk categories, risk scales and evaluation techniques
    d. The budget set aside for potential changes to the scope of the project

44. Which is a type of issue?

    a. A lesson
    b. **A request for change**
    c. An Exception Report
    d. A risk with an estimated high impact

45. What product would enable the Project Manager to review how a Work Package is performing against its cost tolerance?

    a. Configuration Item Record
    b. Quality Register
    c. Highlight Report
    d. **Checkpoint Report**

46. Identify the missing word(s) in the following sentence. PRINCE2 recommends three levels of [?] to reflect the needs of the different levels of management involved in a project.

    a. Management strategies
    b. **Plan**
    c. Stakeholder interests
    d. Time-driven controls

47. Which is NOT a purpose of the Directing a Project process?

    a. Enable the Project Board to be accountable for a project's success by making key decisions
    b. **Enable the Project Board to authorize Work Packages**
    c. Enable the Project Board to delegate day-to-day management of a project to its Project Manager
    d. Enable the Project Board to exercise overall control of a project

48. Which theme defines the accountability for realization of the project's benefits?

    a. Plans
    b. Progress
    c. Organization
    d. Quality

49. Which role is part of the Project Board?

    a. Corporate or programme management
    b. Risk owner
    c. Project Manager
    d. Senior Supplier

50. Which risk response type is appropriate to respond to a threat?

    a. Exploit
    b. Enhance
    c. Reject
    d. Transfer

51. Which of the following is NOT identified in a Product Description?

    a. The quality specification to which a product must be produced
    b. The purpose a product must fulfill
    c. The skills required to undertake quality control of a product
    d. The time and cost tolerances for the creation of a product

52. Identify the missing words in the following sentence. At the end of a stage, the [?] should be used to check whether there is a requirement to send copies of the End Stage Report to external interested parties.

    a. Stage Plan
    b. Communication Management Strategy
    c. Follow-on action recommendations
    d. Quality Management Strategy

53. Which theme provides the controls to escalate any forecast beyond tolerance to the next management level?

  a. Business Case
  b. Plans
  c. Progress
  d. Quality

54. Which provides a single source of reference that may be used by people joining a project after it has been initiated so they can quickly and easily find out how the project is being managed?

  a. Project Brief
  b. Project Initiation Documentation
  c. Project mandate
  d. Project Product Description

55. During the Initiating a Project process, which product is updated to incorporate the estimated time and costs from the Project Plan?

  a. Project Product Description
  b. Business Case
  c. Project Brief
  d. Project mandate

56. Which is a purpose of the Risk theme?

  a. Establish a procedure to ensure every change is agreed by the relevant authority before it takes place
  b. Establish a cost-effective procedure to identify, assess and control uncertainty
  c. Establish mechanisms to control any unacceptable deviations from plan
  d. Establish mechanisms to manage risks at the corporate or programme level of an organization

57. Which is a benefit of using PRINCE2?

    a. Provides a defined structure of accountability, delegation, authority and communication
    b. Includes techniques for critical path analysis and earned value analysis
    c. Enables a Project Manager to be accountable for the success of a project
    d. Prevents any changes once the scope of a project has been agreed

58. Who carries out audits that are independent of the project?

    a. Quality assurance
    b. Project Assurance
    c. Project Support
    d. Project Manager

59. Which is a task of product-based planning?

    a. Design the plan
    b. Create the product flow diagram
    c. Analyze the risks
    d. Prepare the schedule

60. What theme establishes the mechanisms to judge whether a project is worthwhile investing in?

    a. Plans
    b. Business Case
    c. Risk
    d. Quality

61. If a project's benefit tolerance is forecast to be exceeded, to whom should this be escalated to for a decision?

    a. Senior User
    b. Executive
    c. Corporate/programme management
    d. Senior Supplier

62. Which does the Executive need to ensure is in place before the project is initiated?

    a. All Work Packages are authorized
    b. An understanding of how the project will contribute to corporate objectives
    c. The Project Plan has been approved
    d. The Project Initiation Documentation is complete

63. Which is a purpose of the Starting up a Project process?

    a. Provide information so a decision can be made as to whether a project is viable and worthwhile to initiate
    b. Define the means of communication between the project and corporate or programme management
    c. Define the project controls
    d. Record any identified risks in the Risk Register

64. Which is a purpose of the 'Plan' step within the recommended risk management procedure?

    a. Identify the roles and responsibilities for all risk management activities
    b. Prepare and agree the Risk Management Strategy with the Project Board
    c. Plan the Communication Management Strategy to keep stakeholders updated on the risk management activities
    d. Identify possible responses to be implemented to manage a risk should it occur

65. Which describes risk impact?

    a. Timeframe within which the risk might occur
    b. The trigger that occurred giving rise to the risk
    c. The effect of the risk on the delivery of project objectives
    d. How likely the risk is to occur in a given project situation

66. What process ensures focus on the delivery of a stage's products and avoids uncontrolled change?

   a. Directing a Project
   b. Managing a Stage Boundary
   c. Controlling a Stage
   d. Starting up a Project

67. Which is a difference between management and technical stages?

   a. Management stages require planning and technical stages do not
   b. Technical stages can overlap and management stages cannot
   c. Management stages deliver products and technical stages do not
   d. Technical stages require resources and management stages do not

68. Which should be funded from a change budget?

   a. The Starting up a Project process
   b. A fallback plan
   c. An agreed change to the scope of a project
   d. A change to a plan, within allocated tolerances, due to poor estimating

69. Which is a true statement about PRINCE2 event-driven controls?

   a. Event-driven controls take place at predefined periodic intervals
   b. Event-driven controls are produced at the frequency defined in a Work Package
   c. Event-driven controls are used for decision making
   d. Checkpoint Reports are event-driven controls

70. What theme estimates the cost of delivering the project?

   a. Business Case
   b. Change
   c. Plans
   d. Progress

71. What takes place during the Closing a Project process?

    a. The post-project benefits reviews are performed
    b. **Ownership of the project's products is transferred to the customer**
    c. An End Stage Report is prepared for the final stage
    d. The project closure notification is reviewed and approved

72. Which is an objective of the quality review technique?

    a. **To provide confirmation that a product is complete and ready for approval**
    b. To identify solutions to defects found during the quality review meeting
    c. To agree the quality criteria for the product under review
    d. To enable changes to be agreed and added to a baselined product

73. Which is an objective of the Directing a Project process?

    a. Review and approve a project mandate
    b. **Ensure corporate or programme management has an interface to the project**
    c. Define how risks, issues and changes will be managed
    d. Obtain approval for completed products

74. Which is a purpose of the Closing a Project process?

    a. Authorize the final stage of the project
    b. Confirm that all benefits defined in the Business Case have been achieved
    c. **Recognize that objectives set out in the original Project Initiation Documentation have been achieved**
    d. Delegate day-to-day management of the end of the project to the Project Manager

75. Identify the missing word in the following sentence. A risk consists of the [?] of a threat occurring and its impact.

    a. outcome
    b. **probability**
    c. dis-benefit
    d. proximity

Sample Paper - 3

The Foundation Examination

Multiple Choice

1-hour paper

Instructions

1. All 75 questions should be attempted.

2. 5 of the 75 questions are under trial and will not contribute to your overall score. There is no indication of which questions are under trial.

3. All answers are to be marked on the answer sheet provided.

4. Please use a pencil and NOT ink to mark your answers on the answer sheet provided. There is only one correct answer per question.

5. You have 1 hour for this paper.

6. You must get 35 or more correct to pass.

Candidate Number: ....…

1. Which product keeps track of Requests for Change?

a. Request Log
b. Daily Log
c. Quality Log
d. Issue Log

2. In PRINCE2 what product is used to define the information that justifies the setting up, continuation or termination of the project?

a. Project Initiation Document
b. Business Case
c. End Stage Approval
d. Project Brief

3. What provision in Planning can be made for implementing Requests for Change?

a. Project and stage tolerances
b. Contingency plans
c. A Change Budget
d. Adding a contingency margin to estimates

4. Fill in the missing phrase from " a project is a management environment that is Created for the purpose of delivering one or more business products according to ......"

a. The Customer's Needs
b. An Agreed Contract
c. The Project Plan
d. A specified Business Case

5. In what sequence would the (a) Project Initiation Document, (b) the Project Mandate and (c) the Project Brief appear in a PRINCE2 project?

a. a, b, c
b. b, c, a
c. c, a, b
d. c, b, a

6. Which would require the production of an Exception Report?

a. When a Project Issue is received

b. When a Project Board member raises a complaint
c. When a Request For Change or Off-Specification has been received
d. When the current forecasts for the end of the stage deviate beyond the delegated tolerance bounds

7. Which statement is NOT a fundamental principle of "Closing a Project"? "A clear end to a project" –

a. provides a useful opportunity to take stock of achievements
b. provides an opportunity to ensure that all unachieved goals and objectives are identified
c. provides the opportunity to evaluate achievement of all the expected benefits
d. is always more successful than the natural tendency to drift into operational Management

8. What is the more common term used in PRINCE2™ for "deliverable"?

a. Item
b. Package
c. Product
d. Component

9. Which of these items does NOT involve the Project Board?

a. Exception Assessment
b. Highlight Reports
c. Project Closure
d. Work Package Authorization

10. What name is given to the permissible deviation from a plan allowed without immediate reporting to the Project Board?

a. Allowance
b. Contingency
c. Concession
d. Tolerance

11. What other control is closely linked with configuration management?

a. Risk Management
b. Project Closure
c. Change Control
d. Project Initiation

12. Which of these processes does NOT trigger the Planning (PL) process?

a. Starting Up a Project (SU)
b. Initiating a Project (IP)
c. Managing Stage Boundaries (SB)
d. Controlling a Stage (CS)

13. In a Product Breakdown Structure what category of product is a Highlight Report?

a. Quality
b. Specialist
c. Technical
d. Management

14. If, after a Quality Review Follow-up Action, an error is still not resolved, what action should be taken?

a. An Exception Report is made
b. A Project Issue is raised
c. An Exception Memo is raised
d. The review is reconvened

15. Which of the following is NOT a PRINCE2 definition of a project?

a. Has an organization structure
b. Produces defined and measurable business products
c. Uses a defined amount of resources
d. Uses a defined set of techniques

16. What environment does PRINCE2 assume?

a. A fixed-PRICE contract
b. A Customer/Supplier environment
c. A specialist environment
d. A third-party environment

17. Which feature of PRINCE2 tells the Project Manager where a product is, what its status is and who is working on it?

a. Work Package
b. Product Description
c. Checkpoint Report
d. Configuration Management

18. In "Closing a Project" (CP) the project files are archived. What is the explanation? Given for this?

a. To provide useful lessons to future projects
b. Never throw anything away.
c. This material may be needed by Programme Management
d. To permit any future audit of the project's actions

19. Which of the following statements is FALSE? Project Managers using PRINCE2™ are encouraged to …

a. Establish terms of reference as a prerequisite to the start of the project
b. Use a defined structure for delegation, authority and communication
c. Divide the project into manageable stages for more accurate planning
d. Provide brief reports to management at regular meetings

20. Which of these is NOT a valid Risk Management action?

a. Prevention
b. Denial
c. Reduction
d. Transference

21. Which one of these is NOT a PRINCE2 Component?

a. Plans
b. Controls
c. Work Package
d. Configuration Management

22. Which document lists the major products of a plan with their key delivery dates?

a. Product Outline
b. Product Breakdown Structure
c. Checkpoint Report
d. Product Checklist

23. The configuration of the final deliverable of the project is –

a. The sum total of its products

b. The interim products
   c. Its product description
   d. The single end-product

24. Which part of a product lifespan is not part of a project life cycle in the eyes of PRINCE2?

   a. The change-over to operational use of the product
   b. Assessment of the value of the product after a period of use
   c. The specification of the product
   d. Finalization of the business case

25. What is the first job carried out on receipt of a new Project Issue?

   a. Allocation of priority
   b. Logging
   c. Decision on what type of issue
   d. Impact Analysis

26. Which of these statements is FALSE?

   a. The Project Plan is an overview of the total project.
   b. For each stage identified in the Project Plan, a Stage Plan is required.
   c. An Exception Plan needs the approval of the next higher level of authority.
   d. A Team Plan needs approval by the Project Board.

27. Which of the following statements is FALSE?

   a. Customer quality expectations should be discovered in the process "Starting Up a Project"
   b. A company's QMS becomes part of PRINCE2
   c. PRINCE2 may form part of a company's QMS
   d. The Stage Plan describes in detail how part of the Project Plan will be carried out

28. Which one of these statements describes the true purpose of Acceptance Criteria?

   a. A justification for undertaking the project based on estimated costs and anticipated benefits.
   b. A measurable definition of what must be done for the final product to be acceptable to the Customer.
   c. To provide a full and firm foundation for the initiation of a project.
   d. To trigger 'Starting up a Project'.

29. How often does PRINCE2 recommend that open Project Issues should be reviewed?

a. Weekly
b. At Exception Assessments
c. At Checkpoint Meetings
d. On a regular basis

30. What other product is reviewed at the end of each stage apart from the Business Case and Project Plan?

a. The Project Mandate
b. The Team Plan
c. The Risk Log
d. The Project Brief

31. Why is a copy of the Project Issue always returned to the author?

a) The author owns it.
b) To acknowledge its receipt and entry into the system.
c) To elicit further information.
d) To notify rejection of the Issue.

32. Which of the options below reviews the benefits achieved by the project?

a) Post-Project Review
b) Post-Project Review Plan
c) End Project Report
d) Follow-on Action Recommendations

33. Which of these statements is FALSE?

a) A PRINCE2™ project has a finite life span
b) A PRINCE2 project has a defined amount of resources
c) A PRINCE2 project may have only activities, i.e. no products
d) A PRINCE2 project has an organization structure with defined responsibilities, to manage the project

34. The person best situated to keep an eye on a risk is called it's …?

a) Supporter
b) Monitor
c) Owner
d) Librarian

35. Which document reviews actual achievements against the Project Initiation Document?

a) End Project Report

b) Post-Project Review
c) Lessons Learned Report
d) Follow-On Action Recommendations

36. In PRINCE2 all potential changes are dealt with as …?

a) Configuration items
b) Requests For Change
c) Project Issues
d) Exception Reports
e) Action items

37. Which one of these is NOT a key criterion for producing a Product Flow Diagram?

a) Are the products clearly and unambiguously defined?
b) On what other products is each product dependent?
c) Is any product dependant on a product outside the scope of this plan?
d) Which products can be developed in parallel?

38. For a Quality Review, when are suitable reviewers identified?

   a. When the product is passed to configuration management
   b. In the Project Quality Plan
   c. During the QR preparation step
   d. In planning the relevant stage

39. The existence of what product is checked in "Starting up a Project" and its initial version finalized in "Initiating a Project"?

   a. The Project Mandate
   b. The Project Plan
   c. The Project Brief
   d. The Business Case

40. Which does PRINCE2 regard as the third project interest, given user and supplier as the other two?

   a. Technical
   b. Management
   c. Business
   d. Quality

41. PRINCE2 lists a number of reasons why it is seldom desirable or possible to plan an entire project in detail at the start. Which of these is NOT one of these reasons?

   a. A changing or uncertain environment
   b. A PRINCE2 requirement
   c. Difficulty in predicting business conditions in the future
   d. Difficulty in predicting resource availability well into the future

42. In which process is the Project Brief produced?

   a. Starting Up a Project
   b. Initiating a Project
   c. Authorizing Initiation
   d. Authorizing a Project

43. When should a Product Description be baselined?

   a. As soon as it is available in draft form
   b. When the associated product has passed its quality check
   c. When the plan containing its creation is baselined
   d. As soon as it is written

44. An Exception Plan covers what period?

   a. From the problem to the end of the project
   b. From the problem to the end of a plan that will no longer finish within agreed tolerances
   c. The work needed to put the project back within its tolerances
   d. The time needed to produce an Exception Report

45. There are several benefits that the end stage assessment brings to a project. Which one of the following is NOT a benefit?

   a. To enable the approval of an Exception Report
   b. To provide a review of a risky project at key moments when new information about those risks appears
   c. To ensure that key decisions are made prior to the detailed work needed to implement them
   d. To provide a 'fire break' for the project by encouraging the Project Board to assess the project viability at regular intervals

46. The initial Project Plan is based on the Project Brief, the Project Quality Plan and which other product?

a. The Project Approach
   b. The Project Initiation Document
   c. The project start-up notification
   d. The Project Mandate

47. Which document is a record of some current or forecast failure to meet a requirement?

   a. Exception Report
   b. Off-Specification
   c. Follow-On Action Recommendations
   d. Highlight Report

48. If there is a request to change a baselined product, and the change can be done within the stage or Work Package tolerances, how can the decision to implement the change be made?

   a. Project Manager's decision
   b. Team Manager's decision
   c. Team member's decision to who the work has been allocated
   d. Formal change control

49. "Controlling a Stage" drives which other process on a frequent, iterative basis?

   a. Managing Stage Boundaries
   b. Approving a Stage or Exception Plan
   c. Managing Product Delivery
   d. Planning

50. The Project Quality Plan is written in which process?

   a. Initiating a Project
   b. Starting up a Project
   c. Managing Stage Boundaries
   d. Directing a Project

51. What are defined as "partitions of the project with decision points"?

   a. Work Packages
   b. Product Descriptions
   c. Quality Reviews
   d. Stages

52. In which lower level process of "Controlling a Stage" is the Risk Log updated?

   a. Reporting Highlights

b. Assessing Progress
   c. Capturing Project Issues
   d. Examining Project Issues

53. If a question arises on why a particular product was changed, which element of PRINCE2 would be of most help in finding the information?

   a. Issue Log
   b. Quality Log
   c. Configuration Management
   d. Change Control

54. In which sub-process is a Stage Plan updated with actuals?

   a. Assessing Progress
   b. Reviewing Stage Status
   c. Planning a Stage
   d. Reporting Highlights

55. In which sub-process are Checkpoint Reports created?

   a. Executing a Work Package
   b. Assessing Progress
   c. Reporting Highlights
   d. Reviewing Stage Status

56. Are the following statements true or false?

1. Delegated Project Assurance roles report directly to corporate or programme management
2. In PRINCE2 the Project Manager role must be full time
3. A project management structure is a temporary structure

   a. All three are false
   b. Only the third is true
   c. Only the first is false
   d. The second and third are true

57. The process, "Directing a Project" begins when?

   a. From "Starting up a Project"

b. After the start-up of the project
c. At the end of the Initiation Stage
d. Before start-up of the project

58. Apart from "Initiating a Project" in which process is the Business Case updated?

a. Managing Product Delivery
b. Controlling a Stage
c. Managing Stage Boundaries
d. Authorizing a Stage

59. The existence of what information is expected by the process "Starting Up a Project"?

a. A Project Plan
b. A Project Mandate
c. An appointed organization
d. Project Initiation Document

60. In the PRINCE2 document management structure, how many types of file are recommended?

a. One for each Stage
b. Two, Management and Specialist
c. Just the Quality File
d. Three; project, stages and quality

61. In a Quality Review which role does PRINCE2 suggest must ensure that all reviewers are provided with the relevant review products?

a. Producer
b. Scribe
c. Review Chairperson
d. Configuration Librarian

62. Which of these is mandatory in a PRINCE2 project?

a. The use of Team Managers
b. The use of Exception Plans
c. The use of Stages
d. The use of Product Checklists

63. The Project Board has three responsibilities towards the management of risk. Which of the following options is the FALSE one?

a. Notifying the Project Manager of any external risk exposure to the project
b. Making decisions on recommended reactions to risk
c. Identifying, recording and regularly reviewing risks
d. Striking a balance between levels of risk and potential benefits

64. What function creates, maintains and monitors the use of a quality system?

a. Project Support
b. Quality Planning
c. Quality Control
d. Quality assurance

65. Which is NOT a purpose of configuration management?

a. To identify products
b. To create products
c. To track products
d. To protect products

66. Which step is NOT part of "Accepting a Work Package"?

a. Understand the reporting requirements
b. Agree tolerance margins for the Work Package
c. Monitor and control the risks associated with the Work Package
d. Produce a Team Plan which shows that the Work Package can be completed within the constraints

67. Which process provides the information needed for the Project Board to assess the continuing viability of the project?

a. Starting up a Project
b. Closing a Project
c. Planning
d. Managing Stage Boundaries

68. Which of the following are described in the Communication Plan?

1. Who needs information?
2. What information they need
3. Why they need it
4. The format in which it should be presented.

a. The fourth is wrong
b. All four are correct
c. Only the first two are correct
d. The third is wrong.

69. In which process are decisions made on Exception Reports?

a. Managing Stage Boundaries
b. Closing a Project
c. Directing a Project
d. Managing Product Delivery

70. Which process checks for changes to the project management team?

a. Starting up a Project
b. Managing Stage Boundaries
c. Closing a Project
d. Directing a Project

71. From the products listed, which one is produced during 'Starting Up a Project'?

a. The Project Initiation Document
b. The Project Plan
c. The Project Quality Plan
d. The Project Approach

72. Quality responsibilities, both within and external to the project, are defined in which process?

a. Initiating a Project
b. Starting up a Project
c. Managing Stage Boundaries
d. Directing a Project

73. Acceptance for the completed products is obtained as part of which process?

a. Closing a Project
b. Managing Product Delivery
c. Managing Stage Boundaries
d. Controlling a Stage

74. An Exception Report is produced in which sub-process?

a. Taking Corrective Action
b. Reviewing Stage Status
c. Escalating Project Issues
d. Reporting Highlights

75 Which of the following are functions of the start-up process, SU?

1. Setting up the project management team
2. Developing the Project Mandate into the Project Brief
3. Confirming the Project Approach
4. Creating the Issue Log

a. All four
b. the first three
c. the first two
d. the third is wrong

Note - Answers to Sample Questions (Sample Paper 3) are in bold

1. Which product keeps track of Requests for Change?

a. Request Log
b. Daily Log
c. Quality Log
d. Issue Log

2. In PRINCE2 what product is used to define the information that justifies the setting up, continuation or termination of the project?

   a. Project Initiation Document
   b. Business Case
   c. End Stage Approval
   d. Project Brief

3. What provision in Planning can be made for implementing Requests for Change?

   a. Project and stage tolerances
   b. Contingency plans
   c. A Change Budget
   d. Adding a contingency margin to estimates

4. Fill in the missing phrase from " a project is a management environment that is Created for the purpose of delivering one or more business products according to ……"

   a. The Customer's Needs
   b. An Agreed Contract
   c. The Project Plan
   d. A specified Business Case

5. In what sequence would the (a) Project Initiation Document, (b) the Project Mandate and (c) the Project Brief appear in a PRINCE2 project?

   a. a, b, c
   b. b, c, a
   c. c, a, b
   d. c, b, a

6. Which would require the production of an Exception Report?

a. When a Project Issue is received
b. When a Project Board member raises a complaint
c. When a Request For Change or Off-Specification has been received
d. **When the current forecasts for the end of the stage deviate beyond the delegated tolerance bounds**

7. Which statement is NOT a fundamental principle of "Closing a Project"? "A clear end to a project" –

a. provides a useful opportunity to take stock of achievements
b. provides an opportunity to ensure that all unachieved goals and objectives are identified
c. **provides the opportunity to evaluate achievement of all the expected benefits**
d. is always more successful than the natural tendency to drift into operational Management

8. What is the more common term used in PRINCE2™ for "deliverable"?

a. Item
b. Package
c. **Product**
d. Component

9. Which of these items does NOT involve the Project Board?

a. Exception Assessment
b. Highlight Reports
c. Project Closure
d. **Work Package Authorization**

10. What name is given to the permissible deviation from a plan allowed without immediate reporting to the Project Board?

a. Allowance
b. Contingency
c. Concession
d. **Tolerance**

11. What other control is closely linked with configuration management?

a. Risk Management

b. Project Closure
c. **Change Control**
d. Project Initiation

12. Which of these processes does NOT trigger the Planning (PL) process?

a. Starting Up a Project (SU)
b. Initiating a Project (IP)
c. Managing Stage Boundaries (SB)
d. **Controlling a Stage (CS)**

13. In a Product Breakdown Structure what category of product is a Highlight Report?

a. Quality
b. Specialist
c. Technical
d. **Management**

14. If, after a Quality Review Follow-up Action, an error is still not resolved, what action should be taken?

a. An Exception Report is made
b. **A Project Issue is raised**
c. An Exception Memo is raised
d. The review is reconvened

15. Which of the following is NOT a PRINCE2 definition of a project?

a. Has an organization structure
b. Produces defined and measurable business products
c. Uses a defined amount of resources
d. **Uses a defined set of techniques**

16. What environment does PRINCE2 assume?

a. A fixed-PRICE contract
b. **A Customer/Supplier environment**

c. A specialist environment
d. A third-party environment

17. Which feature of PRINCE2 tells the Project Manager where a product is, what its status is and who is working on it?

a. Work Package
b. Product Description
c. Checkpoint Report
d. Configuration Management

18. In "Closing a Project" (CP) the project files are archived. What is the explanation? Given for this?

a. To provide useful lessons to future projects
b. Never throw anything away.
c. This material may be needed by Programme Management
d. To permit any future audit of the project's actions

19. Which of the following statements is FALSE? Project Managers using PRINCE2™ are encouraged to …

a. Establish terms of reference as a prerequisite to the start of the project
b. Use a defined structure for delegation, authority and communication
c. Divide the project into manageable stages for more accurate planning
d. Provide brief reports to management at regular meetings

20. Which of these is NOT a valid Risk Management action?

a. Prevention
b. Denial
c. Reduction
d. Transference

21. Which one of these is NOT a PRINCE2 Component?

a. Plans
b. Controls
c. Work Package
d. Configuration Management

22. Which document lists the major products of a plan with their key delivery dates?

a. Product Outline

b. Product Breakdown Structure
c. Checkpoint Report
d. Product Checklist

23. The configuration of the final deliverable of the project is –

a. The sum total of its products
b. The interim products
c. Its product description
d. The single end-product

24. Which part of a product lifespan is not part of a project life cycle in the eyes of PRINCE2?

a. The change-over to operational use of the product
b. Assessment of the value of the product after a period of use
c. The specification of the product
d. Finalization of the business case

25. What is the first job carried out on receipt of a new Project Issue?

a. Allocation of priority
b. Logging
c. Decision on what type of issue
d. Impact Analysis

26. Which of these statements is FALSE?

a. The Project Plan is an overview of the total project.
b. For each stage identified in the Project Plan, a Stage Plan is required.
c. An Exception Plan needs the approval of the next higher level of authority.
d. A Team Plan needs approval by the Project Board.

27. Which of the following statements is FALSE?

a. Customer quality expectations should be discovered in the process "Starting Up a Project"
b. A company's QMS becomes part of PRINCE2
c. PRINCE2 may form part of a company's QMS
d. The Stage Plan describes in detail how part of the Project Plan will be carried out

28. Which one of these statements describes the true purpose of Acceptance Criteria?

a. A justification for undertaking the project based on estimated costs and anticipated benefits.
b. **A measurable definition of what must be done for the final product to be acceptable to the Customer.**
c. To provide a full and firm foundation for the initiation of a project.
d. To trigger 'Starting up a Project'.

29. How often does PRINCE2 recommend that open Project Issues should be reviewed?

   a. Weekly
   b. At Exception Assessments
   c. At Checkpoint Meetings
   d. **On a regular basis**

30. What other product is reviewed at the end of each stage apart from the Business Case and Project Plan?

   a. The Project Mandate
   b. The Team Plan
   c. **The Risk Log**
   d. The Project Brief

31. Why is a copy of the Project Issue always returned to the author?

a) The author owns it.
b) **To acknowledge its receipt and entry into the system.**
c) To elicit further information.
d) To notify rejection of the Issue.

32. Which of the options below reviews the benefits achieved by the project?

a) **Post-Project Review**
b) Post-Project Review Plan
c) End Project Report
d) Follow-on Action Recommendations

33. Which of these statements is FALSE?

e) A PRINCE2™ project has a finite life span
f) A PRINCE2 project has a defined amount of resources

g) **A PRINCE2 project may have only activities, i.e. no products**
h) A PRINCE2 project has an organization structure with defined responsibilities, to manage the project

34. The person best situated to keep an eye on a risk is called it's …?

a) Supporter
b) Monitor
c) Owner
d) Librarian

35. Which document reviews actual achievements against the Project Initiation Document?

a) End Project Report
b) Post-Project Review
c) Lessons Learned Report
d) Follow-On Action Recommendations

36. In PRINCE2 all potential changes are dealt with as …?

a) Configuration items
b) Requests For Change
c) Project Issues
d) Exception Reports, Action items

37. Which one of these is NOT a key criterion for producing a Product Flow Diagram?

a) Are the products clearly and unambiguously defined?
b) On what other products is each product dependent?
c) Is any product dependant on a product outside the scope of this plan?
d) Which products can be developed in parallel?

38. For a Quality Review, when are suitable reviewers identified?

    e. When the product is passed to configuration management
    f. In the Project Quality Plan
    g. During the QR preparation step
    h. In planning the relevant stage

39. The existence of what product is checked in "Starting up a Project" and its initial version finalized in "Initiating a Project"?

    e. The Project Mandate
    f. The Project Plan
    g. The Project Brief
    h. The Business Case

40. Which does PRINCE2 regard as the third project interest, given user and supplier as the other two?

    e. Technical
    f. Management
    g. Business
    h. Quality

41. PRINCE2 lists a number of reasons why it is seldom desirable or possible to plan an entire project in detail at the start. Which of these is NOT one of these reasons?

    e. A changing or uncertain environment
    f. A PRINCE2 requirement
    g. Difficulty in predicting business conditions in the future
    h. Difficulty in predicting resource availability well into the future

42. In which process is the Project Brief produced?

    e. Starting Up a Project
    f. Initiating a Project
    g. Authorizing Initiation
    h. Authorizing a Project

43. When should a Product Description be baselined?

    e. As soon as it is available in draft form

- f. When the associated product has passed its quality check
- **g. When the plan containing its creation is baselined**
- h. As soon as it is written

44. An Exception Plan covers what period?

- e. From the problem to the end of the project
- **f. From the problem to the end of a plan that will no longer finish within agreed tolerances**
- g. The work needed to put the project back within its tolerances
- h. The time needed to produce an Exception Report

45. There are several benefits that the end stage assessment brings to a project. Which one of the following is NOT a benefit?

- **e. To enable the approval of an Exception Report**
- f. To provide a review of a risky project at key moments when new information about those risks appears
- g. To ensure that key decisions are made prior to the detailed work needed to implement them
- h. To provide a 'fire break' for the project by encouraging the Project Board to assess the project viability at regular intervals

46. The initial Project Plan is based on the Project Brief, the Project Quality Plan and which other product?

- **e. The Project Approach**
- f. The Project Initiation Document
- g. The project start-up notification
- h. The Project Mandate

47. Which document is a record of some current or forecast failure to meet a requirement?

      e. Exception Report
      f. Off-Specification
      g. Follow-On Action Recommendations
      h. Highlight Report

48. If there is a request to change a baselined product, and the change can be done within the stage or Work Package tolerances, how can the decision to implement the change be made?

      e. Project Manager's decision
      f. Team Manager's decision
      g. Team member's decision to who the work has been allocated
      h. Formal change control

49. "Controlling a Stage" drives which other process on a frequent, iterative basis?

      a. Managing Stage Boundaries
      b. Approving a Stage or Exception Plan
      c. Managing Product Delivery
      d. Planning

50. The Project Quality Plan is written in which process?

      a. Initiating a Project
      b. Starting up a Project
      c. Managing Stage Boundaries
      d. Directing a Project

51. What are defined as "partitions of the project with decision points"?

      a. Work Packages

b. Product Descriptions
   c. Quality Reviews
   d. Stages

52. In which lower level process of "Controlling a Stage" is the Risk Log updated?

   a. Reporting Highlights
   b. Assessing Progress
   c. Capturing Project Issues
   d. Examining Project Issues

53. If a question arises on why a particular product was changed, which element of PRINCE2 would be of most help in finding the information?

   a. Issue Log
   b. Quality Log
   c. Configuration Management
   d. Change Control

54. In which sub-process is a Stage Plan updated with actuals?

   e. Assessing Progress
   f. Reviewing Stage Status
   g. Planning a Stage
   h. Reporting Highlights

55. In which sub-process are Checkpoint Reports created?

   e. Executing a Work Package
   f. Assessing Progress
   g. Reporting Highlights
   h. Reviewing Stage Status

56. Are the following statements true or false?

1. Delegated Project Assurance roles report directly to corporate or programme management
2. In PRINCE2 the Project Manager role must be full time
3. A project management structure is a temporary structure

   a. All three are false
   b. Only the third is true
   c. Only the first is false
   d. The second and third are true

57. The process, "Directing a Project" begins when?

   a. From "Starting up a Project"
   b. After the start-up of the project
   c. At the end of the Initiation Stage
   d. Before start-up of the project

58. Apart from "Initiating a Project" in which process is the Business Case updated?

   a. Managing Product Delivery
   b. Controlling a Stage
   c. Managing Stage Boundaries
   d. Authorizing a Stage

59. The existence of what information is expected by the process "Starting Up a Project"?

   a. A Project Plan
   b. A Project Mandate
   c. An appointed organization
   d. Project Initiation Document

60. In the PRINCE2 document management structure, how many types of file are recommended?

   a. One for each Stage
   b. Two, Management and Specialist
   c. Just the Quality File
   d. Three; project, stages and quality

61. In a Quality Review which role does PRINCE2 suggest must ensure that all reviewers are provided with the relevant review products?

   a. Producer
   b. Scribe
   c. Review Chairperson
   d. Configuration Librarian

62. Which of these is mandatory in a PRINCE2 project?

   a. The use of Team Managers
   b. The use of Exception Plans

c. **The use of Stages**
d. The use of Product Checklists

63. The Project Board has three responsibilities towards the management of risk. Which of the following options is the FALSE one?

    a. Notifying the Project Manager of any external risk exposure to the project
    b. Making decisions on recommended reactions to risk
    c. **Identifying, recording and regularly reviewing risks**
    d. Striking a balance between levels of risk and potential benefits

64. What function creates, maintains and monitors the use of a quality system?

    a. Project Support
    b. Quality Planning
    c. Quality Control
    d. **Quality assurance**

65. Which is NOT a purpose of configuration management?

    a. To identify products
    b. **To create products**
    c. To track products
    d. To protect products

66. Which step is NOT part of "Accepting a Work Package"?

    a. Understand the reporting requirements
    b. Agree tolerance margins for the Work Package
    c. **Monitor and control the risks associated with the Work Package**
    d. Produce a Team Plan which shows that the Work Package can be completed within the constraints

67. Which process provides the information needed for the Project Board to assess the continuing viability of the project?

    a. Starting up a Project
    b. Closing a Project
    c. Planning
    d. **Managing Stage Boundaries**

68. Which of the following are described in the Communication Plan?

    1. Who needs information?
    2. What information they need

3. Why they need it
4. The format in which it should be presented.

   a. The fourth is wrong
   b. All four are correct
   c. Only the first two are correct
   d. The third is wrong.

69. In which process are decisions made on Exception Reports?

    a. Managing Stage Boundaries
    b. Closing a Project
    c. Directing a Project
    d. Managing Product Delivery

70. Which process checks for changes to the project management team?

    a. Starting up a Project
    b. Managing Stage Boundaries
    c. Closing a Project
    d. Directing a Project

71. From the products listed, which one is produced during 'Starting Up a Project'?

    a. The Project Initiation Document
    b. The Project Plan
    c. The Project Quality Plan
    d. The Project Approach

72. Quality responsibilities, both within and external to the project, are defined in which process?

a. Initiating a Project
b. Starting up a Project
c. Managing Stage Boundaries
d. Directing a Project

73. Acceptance for the completed products is obtained as part of which process?

a. Closing a Project
b. Managing Product Delivery

c. Managing Stage Boundaries
d. Controlling a Stage

74. An Exception Report is produced in which sub-process?

a. Taking Corrective Action
b. **Reviewing Stage Status**
c. Escalating Project Issues
d. Reporting Highlights

75 Which of the following are functions of the start-up process, SU?

1. Setting up the project management team
2. Developing the Project Mandate into the Project Brief
3. Confirming the Project Approach
4. Creating the Issue Log

a. All four
b. **the first three**
c. the first two
d. the third is wrong

Sample Paper - 4

The Foundation Examination

Multiple Choice

1-hour paper

Instructions

7. All 75 questions should be attempted.

8. 5 of the 75 questions are under trial and will not contribute to your overall score. There is no indication of which questions are under trial.

9. All answers are to be marked on the answer sheet provided.

10. Please use a pencil and NOT ink to mark your answers on the answer sheet provided. There is only one correct answer per question.

11. You have 1 hour for this paper.

12. You must get 35 or more correct to pass.

Candidate Number: ....

1. What process ensures that the project management team is focused on delivery of a stage's products within agreed tolerances?

   a) Directing a Project
   b) Controlling a Stage
   c) Managing a Stage Boundary
   d) Managing Product Delivery

2. Which risk response type is a recommended response to both an opportunity and a threat?
   a) Avoid
   b) Reduce
   c) Share
   d) Reject

3. What process provides the information required to decide whether to authorize the delivery of a project?
   a) Directing a Project
   b) Initiating a Project
   c) Managing Product Delivery
   d) Starting up a Project

4. Which is a benefit of using PRINCE2?
   a) Is a method specifically designed for technical projects
   b) Provides for the efficient and economic use of management time
   c) Includes many of the proven planning techniques, such as critical path analysis
   d) Can be used to manage both projects and programmes

5. Which is a responsibility of Project Support?
   a) Approving or rejecting issues
   b) Setting of stage tolerances
   c) Assessing whether quality control procedures are used correctly
   d) Controlling and protecting the project's products

6. Which is NOT a characteristic of a project?
   a) Introduces business change
   b) Less risky than stable business operations
   c) Involves a team of people with different skills working on a temporary basis
   d) Has a defined start and a defined end date

7. Which project management team member represents the interest of those who will operate the project's products to realize the benefits after the project is complete?

   a) Executive
   b) Senior User
   c) Senior Supplier
   d) Project Manager

8. Which two roles are linked by the Managing Product Delivery process?
   a) Corporate or programme management and Project Board
   b) Project Board and Project Manager
   c) Project Manager and Team Manager
   d) Team Manager and external supplier

9. Which is a purpose of the Project Product Description?
   a) Define the key responsibilities for delivering product quality
   b) Provide information about the state of products
   c) Define the quality anticipated by the customer
   d) Provide product cost input to the Business Case

10. Which regular report provides the Project Board with a summary of stage status?
    a) Communication Management Strategy
    b) Project Brief
    c) Highlight Report
    d) Checkpoint Report

11. Which theme addresses the need to have a strategy for communicating with stakeholders?
    a) Quality
    b) Organization
    c) Plans
    d) Progress

12. What is the collective name for individuals or groups who may be affected by a project?
    a) Customers
    b) Project Support
    c) Stakeholders
    d) Team members

13. If an informal issue is defined as a problem or concern, where should it first be recorded?
    a) Issue Register
    b) Risk Register
    c) Daily Log
    d) Exception Report

14. Which describes risk appetite?
    a) An organization's unique attitude towards risk-taking
    b) The risks to the expected benefits
    c) A common set of risk categories, risk scales and evaluation techniques
    d) The budget set aside for potential changes to the scope of the project

15. How many tasks does the product-based planning technique describe?
    a) One
    b) Two
    c) Three
    d) Four

16. Identify the missing words in the following sentence.
    A Project Manager agrees the [?] with a Team Manager.
    a) project cost tolerance
    b) stage cost tolerance
    c) Work Package cost tolerance
    d) product cost tolerance

17. Which activity should take place before the initiation of a project is authorized?
    a) Assemble the Project Initiation Documentation
    b) Update the Risk Register with any risks
    c) Assemble the Project Brief
    d) Decide if a change budget should be established

18. Which is NOT a purpose of a Benefits Review Plan?
    a) Define the period over which the cost-benefit analysis will be based
    b) Support a review of the performance of the project's products in operational use
    c) Define the scope, timing and ownership of the benefit reviews required
    d) Describe how to measure and confirm benefits after the project is closed

19. Which is an objective of the quality review technique?
    a) To baseline a product
    b) To provide a common understanding of what products a project will create
    c) To define the quality methods required within a project
    d) To determine the quality responsibilities of a project team

20. Which describes a risk event?
    a) The area of uncertainty in terms of the threat or opportunity
    b) The derivation or sources of a potential risk to the project
    c) The achievement of a milestone on the Project Plan
    d) The sequence of events and actions that will be put in place if a risk occurs

21. What should be used to fund a new approved requirement that a Team Manager believes is critical for the success of the project?

    a) Work Package cost tolerance
    b) Fallback plan
    c) Stage cost tolerance
    d) Change budget

22. In which product does a Project Manager define the time and cost tolerances for the work to be done by a Team Manager?
    a) Product Description
    b) Team Plan
    c) Work Package
    d) Stage Plan

23. Which is a true statement about the Change theme?
    a) Change control is only performed at the beginning of each stage
    b) Change control is used to prevent changes to baselined products
    c) Change control is only used on specialist products
    d) Change control is continually performed during the life of a project

24. Which is NOT an objective of the Starting up a Project process?
    a) Ensure the project has sound acceptance criteria
    b) Confirm the key milestones have been correctly selected
    c) Understand the different ways the work of the project can be undertaken
    d) Confirm the definition of the project's scope

25. Which describes the 'Identify Risks' step within the recommended risk management procedure?
    a) Identify responses to risks documented in the Business Case
    b) Gather information about the project environment and objectives
    c) Identify the roles to be involved in risk management activities
    d) Identify uncertainties that may impact on the delivery of the project objectives

26. Which is a recommended quality review team role?
    a) Project Manager
    b) Assurance
    c) Project Support
    d) Administrator

27. What takes place during the Closing a Project process?
    a) The post-project benefits reviews are performed
    b) Ownership of the project's products is transferred to the customer

c) An End Stage Report is prepared for the final stage
d) The project closure notification is reviewed and approved

28. Which is a reason for creating a product flow diagram?
    a) Establish the order in which the products are to be created
    b) Ensure complete understanding of each product's purpose
    c) Document the project approach
    d) Identify start and end dates for the development of each product

29. Which is a purpose of the Risk theme?
    a) Provide the means of recording any complaints from stakeholders
    b) Establish a procedure that enables proactive identification, assessing and controlling of risks
    c) Identify, assess and control any approved changes to the baseline
    d) Prepare the organization's risk management policy

30. What plan is created, and submitted for approval, during the Managing a Stage Boundary process?
    a) Team Plan
    b) Stage Plan
    c) Benefits Review Plan
    d) Project Plan

31. Which of the following apply to a project outcome?
    a) It is used to identify the management products for the project
    b) It is the result of the change derived from using the project's outputs
    c) If perceived as an advantage by one or more stakeholders, it results in a benefit
    d) If perceived as negative by one or more stakeholders, it results in a dis-benefit

    a) 1, 2, 3
    b) 1, 2, 4
    c) 1, 3, 4
    d) 2, 3, 4

32. Which is a purpose of quality planning?
    a) Define the structure of the project management team
    b) Detail the acceptance criteria, in order for the Project Board to agree the level of quality expected of the project's product
    c) Document approval records for those project products that have met their quality criteria
    d) Produce the Project Plan with resource and schedule information

33. What product records any time tolerances agreed between the Project Manager and Team Manager?
    a) Product Description
    b) Work Package
    c) Project Initiation Documentation
    d) Stage Plan

34. What is used to identify any organization or interested party who needs to be informed of project closure?
    a) Configuration Management Strategy
    b) Project management team structure
    c) Communication Management Strategy
    d) Project Brief

35. A product can NOT be supplied to meet all of the requirements in its baselined Product Description. What first action should be taken?
    a) Raise a request for change
    b) Raise an off-specification
    c) Write an Exception Report
    d) Amend the Work Package

36. Which product summarizes progress and is used to decide whether to amend the project scope or stop the project?
    a) Checkpoint Report
    b) End Stage Report
    c) End Project Report
    d) Product Status Account

37. Which is a purpose of the Starting up a Project process?
    a) Provide information so a decision can be made as to whether a project is viable and worthwhile to initiate
    b) Define the means of communication between the project and corporate or programme
       Management
    c) Define the project controls
    d) Record any identified risks in the Risk Register

38. Which is a type of issue?
    a) A lesson
    b) A request for change
    c) An Exception Report
    d) A risk with an estimated high impact

39. What product might a Project Manager request to identify any variation between reported progress and actual progress?
    a) Product Status Account
    b) Stage Plan
    c) Issue Register
    d) Daily Log

40. When considering how long the project stages should be, which might be a reason for one stage to be longer than others?
    a) A substantial amount of the project budget is to be spent
    b) More human resources are required than in other stages
    c) The risk is lower
    d) No changes to the project management team are envisaged

41. Who carries out audits that are independent of the project?
    a) Quality assurance
    b) Project Assurance
    c) Project Support
    d) Project Manager

42. Identify the missing words in the following sentence. A purpose of the [?] process is to assign work to a Team Manager.
    a) Controlling a Stage
    b) Directing a Project
    c) Managing a Stage Boundary
    d) Managing Product Delivery

43. Which PRINCE2 integrated element describes the guiding obligations and good practices which determine whether a project is genuinely being managed using PRINCE2?
    a) Principles
    b) Processes
    c) Tailoring PRINCE2 to the project environment
    d) Themes

44. Which is a typical core activity within a configuration management procedure?
    a) Quality assurance
    b) Risk management
    c) Verification and audit
    d) Progress reporting

45. When considering risks, which describes an opportunity in a project?
    a) An uncertain event that could have a negative impact on objectives
    b) An uncertain event that could have a favorable impact on objectives
    c) An event that has occurred resulting in a negative impact on objectives
    d) An event that has occurred resulting in a favorable impact on objectives

46. Which is an objective of the Directing a Project process?
    a) Create and authorize the project mandate
    b) Provide management control and direction
    c) Control the day-to-day running of the project
    d) Provide accurate progress information to the Project Manager

47. Which action should be taken within the Closing a Project process to ensure benefits that still need to be realized are measured?
    a) Prevent closure of a project until all benefits are realized
    b) Update a Benefits Review Plan with the dates of post-project benefits reviews
    c) Create a follow-on action recommendation for each benefit yet to be measured
    d) Make the role of Project Manager responsible for the measurement of benefits once a project is closed

48. What is a purpose of a Benefits Review Plan?
    a) Provide information regarding unfinished work to the group which will support the project's products in their operational life
    b) Give a detailed analysis of only those benefits that were realized before the project closed
    c) Document the justification for undertaking the project, based on the estimated costs versus the anticipated benefits
    d) Provide details of the time and effort needed to carry out the planned benefits reviews

49. Which statement applies to Stage Plans?
    a) Always have the same duration as the Project Plan
    b) Are produced at the same time as the Project Initiation Documentation
    c) Assist the Project Manager in the day-to-day running and control of the project
    d) Provide a baseline against which the Project Board monitor overall progress

50. Which is a purpose of the Plans theme?
    a) Identify, assess and control uncertainty within the project
    b) Establish a coding system for all components of the project's products
    c) Define the means of delivering the products
    d) Produce a Benefits Review Plan

51. What theme establishes the mechanisms to judge whether a project is worthwhile investing in?
    a) Plans
    b) Business Case
    c) Risk
    d) Quality

52. Which role is part of the Project Board?
    a) Corporate or programme management
    b) Risk owner
    c) Project Manager
    d) Senior Supplier

53. Which process provides the Project Board with the information it requires in order to commit resources to the project?
    a) Managing Product Delivery
    b) Initiating a Project
    c) Controlling a Stage
    d) Directing a Project

54. Which is a purpose of the Quality theme?

    a) Establish how the project will ensure that all products created meet their requirements
    b) Establish quality assurance to maintain the quality management system
    c) Identify all the products of the project to ensure the scope has been adequately defined
    d) Determine the communication needs of the organization's quality assurance function

55. Which aspect of project performance must be managed to ensure the project's products are fit for purpose?
    a) Benefits
    b) Quality
    c) Risk
    d) Scope

56. Which is a purpose of the Closing a Project process?
    a) Provide a fixed point at which acceptance for the project product is confirmed
    b) Receive the completed Work Packages for the work performed in the final stage
    c) Identify who will perform the activities to close a project
    d) Recognize that the objectives set out in the original Project Brief have been achieved

57. Identify the missing word(s) in the following sentence. PRINCE2 recommends three levels of [?] to reflect the needs of the different levels of Management involved in a project.
    a) Management strategies
    b) Plan
    c) Stakeholder interests
    d) Time-driven controls

58. Which is NOT a purpose of the Progress theme?
    a) To monitor and compare actual achievement against those planned
    b) To define the means of delivering products
    c) To control any unacceptable deviation
    d) To provide a forecast for the project objectives and the project's continued viability

59. Identify the missing product in the following sentence. When assessing an issue during the Controlling a Stage process, the [?] provides essential information to evaluate the viability of the project.

    a) Project Brief
    b) Benefits Review Plan
    c) Project Initiation Documentation
    d) Configuration Management Strategy

60. Which of the following are true statements about the Lessons Report?
    1. Used to pass on lessons that may be applied to other projects
    2. Can be produced at any time during the project
    3. Identifies when post-project benefits reviews will be held
    4. The supplier may have a separate Lessons Report than the rest of the project

    a) 1, 2, 3
    b) 1, 2, 4
    c) 1, 3, 4
    d) 2, 3, 4

61. Which product describes the roles and responsibilities for achieving the effective management? Of anticipated threats and opportunities in a project?
    a) Quality Management Strategy
    b) Risk Management Strategy
    c) Communication Management Strategy
    d) Configuration Management Strategy

62. Which role is assigned to carry out a risk response action but is NOT responsible for managing all aspects of a particular risk?
    a) Project Manager
    b) Risk owner
    c) Risk actionee
    d) Project Support

63. Identify the missing words in the following sentence. The Managing a Stage Boundary process should be executed [?] a management stage.
    a) when a Stage Plan has been prepared for
    b) at the beginning of
    c) when all the technical stages have been completed within
    d) at, or close to the end of,

64. Which of the following is NOT identified when estimating a risk?
    a) Likelihood of each risk occurring
    b) Potential impact on the project delivering its objectives
    c) When during the lifetime of the project the risk might occur
    d) Estimated cost of response actions

65. Which is a responsibility of the managing level within the project management team?
    a) Set project tolerances
    b) Approve stage completion
    c) Ensure that the products are produced within the constraints agreed with the Project Board
    d) Design and appoint the project management team

66. Which is a purpose of the Directing a Project process?
    a) Create and authorize the project mandate
    b) Ensure that work on products allocated to the team is authorized and agreed
    c) Control the day-to-day running of the project
    d) Delegate day-to-day management of the project to the Project Manager

67. Which of the following are true statements about the Directing a Project process?
1. Provides the Project Brief
2. Starts at the end of the Starting up a Project process
3. Provides a mechanism for the Project Board to assure that a project has continued business justification
4. Enables the Project Board to provide informal advice and guidance as well as formal Direction

    a) 1, 2, 3
    b) 1, 2, 4
    c) 1, 3, 4
    d) 2, 3, 4

68. What principle is supported by the Project Board representing the primary stakeholder interests?
    a) Manage by stages
    b) Focus on products
    c) Defined roles and responsibilities
    d) Learn from experience

69. Where should a Team Manager look for information on the quality required for a product?
    a) Project Initiation Documentation
    b) Product Description
    c) Team Plan
    d) Quality Management Strategy

70. Which theme provides the controls to escalate any forecast beyond tolerance to the next management level?
    a) Business Case
    b) Plans
    c) Progress
    d) Quality

71. Identify the missing words in the following sentence PRINCE2 is based on [?] environment.
    a) a corporate or programme management
    b) a customer/supplier
    c) an external supplier
    d) a stakeholder

72. What process provides progress information on a team's work to the Project Manager?
    a) Controlling a Stage
    b) Directing a Project
    c) Managing a Stage Boundary
    d) Managing Product Delivery

73. Which process provides the Project Board with sufficient information for it to review the success of a completed stage and confirm continued business justification?
    a) Controlling a Stage
    b) Closing a Project
    c) Directing a Project
    d) Managing a Stage Boundary

74. Which may be funded from a risk budget?
    a) Corrections due to off-specifications
    b) Impact analysis of requests for change
    c) Implementation of a fallback plan
    d) Preparation of the Risk Management Strategy

75. Which is a true statement about time-driven controls?
    a) Time-driven controls are used for monitoring the progress of Work Packages and management stages
    b) Time-driven controls take place when specific events happen
    c) Time-driven controls are produced at the end of a stage
    d) An Exception Report is a time-driven control

Note - Answers to Sample Questions (Sample Paper 4) are in bold

1. What process ensures that the project management team is focused on delivery of a stage's products within agreed tolerances?

    a) Directing a Project
    b) Controlling a Stage
    c) Managing a Stage Boundary
    d) Managing Product Delivery

2. Which risk response type is a recommended response to both an opportunity and a threat?
    a) Avoid
    b) Reduce
    c) Share
    d) Reject

3. What process provides the information required to decide whether to authorize the delivery of a project?
    a) Directing a Project
    b) Initiating a Project
    c) Managing Product Delivery
    d) Starting up a Project

4. Which is a benefit of using PRINCE2?
    a) Is a method specifically designed for technical projects
    b) Provides for the efficient and economic use of management time
    c) Includes many of the proven planning techniques, such as critical path analysis
    d) Can be used to manage both projects and programmes

5. Which is a responsibility of Project Support?
    a) Approving or rejecting issues
    b) Setting of stage tolerances
    c) Assessing whether quality control procedures are used correctly
    d) Controlling and protecting the project's products

6. Which is NOT a characteristic of a project?
   a) Introduces business change
   b) **Less risky than stable business operations**
   c) Involves a team of people with different skills working on a temporary basis
   d) Has a defined start and a defined end date

7. Which project management team member represents the interest of those who will operate the project's products to realize the benefits after the project is complete?

   a) Executive
   b) **Senior User**
   c) Senior Supplier
   d) Project Manager

8. Which two roles are linked by the Managing Product Delivery process?
   a) Corporate or programme management and Project Board
   b) Project Board and Project Manager
   c) **Project Manager and Team Manager**
   d) Team Manager and external supplier

9. Which is a purpose of the Project Product Description?
   a) Define the key responsibilities for delivering product quality
   b) Provide information about the state of products
   c) **Define the quality anticipated by the customer**
   d) Provide product cost input to the Business Case

10. Which regular report provides the Project Board with a summary of stage status?
    a) Communication Management Strategy
    b) Project Brief
    c) **Highlight Report**
    d) Checkpoint Report

11. Which theme addresses the need to have a strategy for communicating with stakeholders?
    a) Quality
    b) Organization
    c) Plans
    d) Progress

12. What is the collective name for individuals or groups who may be affected by a project?
    a) Customers
    b) Project Support
    c) Stakeholders
    d) Team members

13. If an informal issue is defined as a problem or concern, where should it first be recorded?
    a) Issue Register
    b) Risk Register
    c) Daily Log
    d) Exception Report

14. Which describes risk appetite?
    a) An organization's unique attitude towards risk-taking
    b) The risks to the expected benefits
    c) A common set of risk categories, risk scales and evaluation techniques
    d) The budget set aside for potential changes to the scope of the project

15. How many tasks does the product-based planning technique describe?
    a) One
    b) Two
    c) Three
    d) Four

16. Identify the missing words in the following sentence. Project Manager agrees the [?] with a Team Manager.
    a) project cost tolerance
    b) stage cost tolerance
    c) Work Package cost tolerance
    d) product cost tolerance

17. Which activity should take place before the initiation of a project is authorized?
    a) Assemble the Project Initiation Documentation
    b) Update the Risk Register with any risks
    c) Assemble the Project Brief
    d) Decide if a change budget should be established

18. Which is NOT a purpose of a Benefits Review Plan?
    a) Define the period over which the cost-benefit analysis will be based
    b) Support a review of the performance of the project's products in operational use
    c) Define the scope, timing and ownership of the benefit reviews required
    d) Describe how to measure and confirm benefits after the project is closed

19. Which is an objective of the quality review technique?
    a) To baseline a product
    b) To provide a common understanding of what products a project will create
    c) To define the quality methods required within a project
    d) To determine the quality responsibilities of a project team

20. Which describes a risk event?
    a) The area of uncertainty in terms of the threat or opportunity
    b) The derivation or sources of a potential risk to the project
    c) The achievement of a milestone on the Project Plan
    d) The sequence of events and actions that will be put in place if a risk occurs

21. What should be used to fund a new approved requirement that a Team Manager believes is critical for the success of the project?

    a) Work Package cost tolerance
    b) Fallback plan
    c) Stage cost tolerance
    d) Change budget

22. In which product does a Project Manager define the time and cost tolerances for the work to be done by a Team Manager?
    a) Product Description
    b) Team Plan
    c) Work Package
    d) Stage Plan

23. Which is a true statement about the Change theme?
    a) Change control is only performed at the beginning of each stage
    b) Change control is used to prevent changes to baselined products
    c) Change control is only used on specialist products
    d) Change control is continually performed during the life of a project

24. Which is NOT an objective of the Starting up a Project process?
    a) Ensure the project has sound acceptance criteria
    b) Confirm the key milestones have been correctly selected
    c) Understand the different ways the work of the project can be undertaken
    d) Confirm the definition of the project's scope

25. Which describes the 'Identify Risks' step within the recommended risk management procedure?
    a) Identify responses to risks documented in the Business Case
    b) Gather information about the project environment and objectives
    c) Identify the roles to be involved in risk management activities
    d) Identify uncertainties that may impact on the delivery of the project objectives

26. Which is a recommended quality review team role?
    a) Project Manager
    b) Assurance
    c) Project Support
    d) Administrator

27. What takes place during the Closing a Project process?
    a) The post-project benefits reviews are performed
    b) **Ownership of the project's products is transferred to the customer**
    c) An End Stage Report is prepared for the final stage
    d) The project closure notification is reviewed and approved

28. Which is a reason for creating a product flow diagram?
    a) **Establish the order in which the products are to be created**
    b) Ensure complete understanding of each product's purpose
    c) Document the project approach
    d) Identify start and end dates for the development of each product

29. Which is a purpose of the Risk theme?
    a) Provide the means of recording any complaints from stakeholders
    b) **Establish a procedure that enables proactive identification, assessing and controlling of risks**
    c) Identify, assess and control any approved changes to the baseline
    d) Prepare the organization's risk management policy

30. What plan is created, and submitted for approval, during the Managing a Stage Boundary process?
    a) Team Plan
    b) **Stage Plan**
    c) Benefits Review Plan
    d) Project Plan

31. Which of the following apply to a project outcome?
    1. It is used to identify the management products for the project
    2. It is the result of the change derived from using the project's outputs
    3. If perceived as an advantage by one or more stakeholders, it results in a benefit
    4. If perceived as negative by one or more stakeholders, it results in a dis-benefit

    a) 1, 2, 3
    b) 1, 2, 4
    c) 1, 3, 4
    d) 2, 3, 4

32. Which is a purpose of quality planning?
    a) Define the structure of the project management team
    b) Detail the acceptance criteria, in order for the Project Board to agree the level of quality expected of the project's product
    c) Document approval records for those project products that have met their quality criteria
    d) Produce the Project Plan with resource and schedule information

33. What product records any time tolerances agreed between the Project Manager and Team Manager?
    a) Product Description
    b) Work Package
    c) Project Initiation Documentation
    d) Stage Plan

34. What is used to identify any organization or interested party who needs to be informed of project closure?
    a) Configuration Management Strategy
    b) Project management team structure
    c) Communication Management Strategy
    d) Project Brief

35. A product can NOT be supplied to meet all of the requirements in its baselined Product Description. What first action should be taken?
   a) Raise a request for change
   b) **Raise an off-specification**
   c) Write an Exception Report
   d) Amend the Work Package

36. Which product summarizes progress and is used to decide whether to amend the project scope or stop the project?
   a) Checkpoint Report
   b) **End Stage Report**
   c) End Project Report
   d) Product Status Account

37. Which is a purpose of the Starting up a Project process?
   a) **Provide information so a decision can be made as to whether a project is viable and worthwhile to initiate**
   b) Define the means of communication between the project and corporate or program Management
   c) Define the project controls
   d) Record any identified risks in the Risk Register

38. Which is a type of issue?
    a) A lesson
    b) A request for change
    c) An Exception Report
    d) A risk with an estimated high impact

39. What product might a Project Manager request to identify any variation between reported progress and actual progress?
    a) Product Status Account
    b) Stage Plan
    c) Issue Register
    d) Daily Log

40. When considering how long the project stages should be, which might be a reason for one stage to be longer than others?
    a) A substantial amount of the project budget is to be spent
    b) More human resources are required than in other stages
    c) The risk is lower
    d) No changes to the project management team are envisaged

41. Who carries out audits that are independent of the project?
    a) Quality assurance
    b) Project Assurance
    c) Project Support
    d) Project Manager

42. Identify the missing words in the following sentence. A purpose of the [?] process is to assign work to a Team Manager.
    a) Controlling a Stage
    b) Directing a Project
    c) Managing a Stage Boundary
    d) Managing Product Delivery

43. Which PRINCE2 integrated element describes the guiding obligations and good practices which determine whether a project is genuinely being managed using PRINCE2?
    a) Principles
    b) Processes
    c) Tailoring PRINCE2 to the project environment
    d) Themes

44. Which is a typical core activity within a configuration management procedure?
    a) Quality assurance
    b) Risk management
    c) Verification and audit
    d) Progress reporting

45. When considering risks, which describes an opportunity in a project?
    a) An uncertain event that could have a negative impact on objectives
    b) An uncertain event that could have a favorable impact on objectives
    c) An event that has occurred resulting in a negative impact on objectives
    d) An event that has occurred resulting in a favorable impact on objectives

46. Which is an objective of the Directing a Project process?
    a) Create and authorize the project mandate
    b) **Provide management control and direction**
    c) Control the day-to-day running of the project
    d) Provide accurate progress information to the Project Manager

47. Which action should be taken within the Closing a Project process to ensure benefits that still need to be realized are measured?
    a) Prevent closure of a project until all benefits are realized
    b) Update a Benefits Review Plan with the dates of post-project benefits reviews
    c) **Create a follow-on action recommendation for each benefit yet to be measured**
    d) Make the role of Project Manager responsible for the measurement of benefits once a project is closed

48. What is a purpose of a Benefits Review Plan?
    a) Provide information regarding unfinished work to the group which will support the project's products in their operational life
    b) Give a detailed analysis of only those benefits that were realized before the project closed
    c) Document the justification for undertaking the project, based on the estimated costs versus the anticipated benefits
    d) **Provide details of the time and effort needed to carry out the planned benefits reviews**

49. Which statement applies to Stage Plans?
    a) Always have the same duration as the Project Plan
    b) Are produced at the same time as the Project Initiation Documentation
    c) **Assist the Project Manager in the day-to-day running and control of the project**
    d) Provide a baseline against which the Project Board monitor overall progress

50. Which is a purpose of the Plans theme?
    a) Identify, assess and control uncertainty within the project
    b) Establish a coding system for all components of the project's products
    c) Define the means of delivering the products
    d) Produce a Benefits Review Plan

51. What theme establishes the mechanisms to judge whether a project is worthwhile investing in?
    a) Plans
    b) Business Case
    c) Risk
    d) Quality

52. Which role is part of the Project Board?
    a) Corporate or programme management
    b) Risk owner
    c) Project Manager
    d) Senior Supplier

53. Which process provides the Project Board with the information it requires in order to commit resources to the project?
    a) Managing Product Delivery
    b) Initiating a Project
    c) Controlling a Stage
    d) Directing a Project

54. Which is a purpose of the Quality theme?

   a) **Establish how the project will ensure that all products created meet their requirements**
   b) Establish quality assurance to maintain the quality management system
   c) Identify all the products of the project to ensure the scope has been adequately defined
   d) Determine the communication needs of the organization's quality assurance function

55. Which aspect of project performance must be managed to ensure the project's products are fit for purpose?
   a) Benefits
   b) **Quality**
   c) Risk
   d) Scope

56. Which is a purpose of the Closing a Project process?
   a) **Provide a fixed point at which acceptance for the project product is confirmed**
   b) Receive the completed Work Packages for the work performed in the final stage
   c) Identify who will perform the activities to close a project
   d) Recognize that the objectives set out in the original Project Brief have been achieved

57. Identify the missing word(s) in the following sentence. PRINCE2 recommends three levels of [?] to reflect the needs of the different levels of Management involved in a project.
   a) Management strategies
   b) **Plan**
   c) Stakeholder interests
   d) Time-driven controls

58. Which is NOT a purpose of the Progress theme?
    a) To monitor and compare actual achievement against those planned
    b) To define the means of delivering products
    c) To control any unacceptable deviation
    d) To provide a forecast for the project objectives and the project's continued viability

59. Identify the missing product in the following sentence. When assessing an issue during the Controlling a Stage process, the [?] provides essential information to evaluate the viability of the project.

    a) Project Brief
    b) Benefits Review Plan
    c) Project Initiation Documentation
    d) Configuration Management Strategy

60. Which of the following are true statements about the Lessons Report?
    1. Used to pass on lessons that may be applied to other projects
    2. Can be produced at any time during the project
    3. Identifies when post-project benefits reviews will be held
    4. The supplier may have a separate Lessons Report than the rest of the project

    a) 1, 2, 3
    b) 1, 2, 4
    c) 1, 3, 4
    d) 2, 3, 4

61. Which product describes the roles and responsibilities for achieving the effective management? Of anticipated threats and opportunities in a project?
    a) Quality Management Strategy
    b) Risk Management Strategy
    c) Communication Management Strategy
    d) Configuration Management Strategy

62. Which role is assigned to carry out a risk response action but is NOT responsible for managing all aspects of a particular risk?
    a) Project Manager
    b) Risk owner
    c) Risk actionee
    d) Project Support

63. Identify the missing words in the following sentence. The Managing a Stage Boundary process should be executed [?] a management stage.
    a) when a Stage Plan has been prepared for
    b) at the beginning of
    c) when all the technical stages have been completed within
    d) at, or close to the end of,

64. Which of the following is NOT identified when estimating a risk?
    a) Likelihood of each risk occurring
    b) Potential impact on the project delivering its objectives
    c) When during the lifetime of the project the risk might occur
    d) Estimated cost of response actions

65. Which is a responsibility of the managing level within the project management team?
    a) Set project tolerances
    b) Approve stage completion
    c) Ensure that the products are produced within the constraints agreed with the Project Board
    d) Design and appoint the project management team

66. Which is a purpose of the Directing a Project process?
    a) Create and authorize the project mandate
    b) Ensure that work on products allocated to the team is authorized and agreed
    c) Control the day-to-day running of the project
    d) Delegate day-to-day management of the project to the Project Manager

67. Which of the following are true statements about the Directing a Project process?
1. Provides the Project Brief
2. Starts at the end of the Starting up a Project process
3. Provides a mechanism for the Project Board to assure that a project has continued business justification
4. Enables the Project Board to provide informal advice and guidance as well as formal Direction

   a) 1, 2, 3
   b) 1, 2, 4
   c) 1, 3, 4
   d) 2, 3, 4

68. What principle is supported by the Project Board representing the primary stakeholder interests?
   a) Manage by stages
   b) Focus on products
   c) Defined roles and responsibilities
   d) Learn from experience

69. Where should a Team Manager look for information on the quality required for a product?
   a) Project Initiation Documentation
   b) Product Description
   c) Team Plan
   d) Quality Management Strategy

70. Which theme provides the controls to escalate any forecast beyond tolerance to the next management level?
   a) Business Case
   b) Plans
   c) Progress
   d) Quality

71. Identify the missing words in the following sentence PRINCE2 is based on [?] environment.
    a) a corporate or programme management
    b) a customer/supplier
    c) an external supplier
    d) a stakeholder

72. What process provides progress information on a team's work to the Project Manager?
    a) Controlling a Stage
    b) Directing a Project
    c) Managing a Stage Boundary
    d) Managing Product Delivery

73. Which process provides the Project Board with sufficient information for it to review the success of a completed stage and confirm continued business justification?
    a) Controlling a Stage
    b) Closing a Project
    c) Directing a Project
    d) Managing a Stage Boundary

74. Which may be funded from a risk budget?
    a) Corrections due to off-specifications
    b) Impact analysis of requests for change
    c) Implementation of a fallback plan
    d) Preparation of the Risk Management Strategy

75. Which is a true statement about time-driven controls?
    a) Time-driven controls are used for monitoring the progress of Work Packages and management stages
    b) Time-driven controls take place when specific events happen
    c) Time-driven controls are produced at the end of a stage
    d) An Exception Report is a time-driven control

Glossary of Terms

Acceptance Criteria	A prioritized list of criteria that the project product must meet before the customer will accept it, i.e. **measurable** definitions of the attributes required for the set of products to be acceptable to key stakeholders
Avoid (risk response)	A risk response to a threat where the threat either can **no** longer have an impact or can no longer happen
Baseline	**Reference levels** against which an entity is monitored and controlled
Benefits Review Plan	A plan that defines how and when a **measurement** of the achievement of the **project's benefits** can be made. If the project is being managed within a programme, this information may be created and maintained at the programme level
Business Case	The **justification** for an organizational activity (project), which typically contains costs, benefits, risks and timescales, and against which continuing **viability** is tested
Change Authority	A person or group to which the Project Board may delegate responsibility for the **consideration of requests for change or off- specifications**. The Change Authority may be given a **change budget** and can approve changes within that budget
Change Budget	The **money** allocated to the **Change Authority** available to be spent on authorized requests for change
Closure Notification	**Advice from the Project Board** to inform all stakeholders and the host sites that the project resources can be disbanded and support services, such as space, equipment and access, demobilized.
Closure Recommendation	A **recommendation** prepared by the Project Manager **for the Project Board** to send as a project closure notification when the board is satisfied that the project can be closed
Communication Management Strategy	A description of the means and frequency of **communication** between the project and the project's **stakeholders**

Concession	An **off-specification** that is **accepted** by the Project Board without corrective action
Configuration Item Record	A record that describes the **status, version** and variant of a configuration item, and any details of important relationships between them
Configuration Management Strategy	A description of how and by whom the project's **products** will be **controlled** and protected
Constraints	The restrictions or **limitations** that the project is bound by
Cost Tolerance	The **permissible deviation** in a plan's **cost** that is allowed before the deviation needs to be escalated to the next level of management
Daily Log	Used to **record** problems/concerns that can be handled by the **Project Manager informally**
End Project Report	A **report** given by the Project Manager to the Project Board, that confirms the **handover** of all **products** and provides an updated Business Case and an assessment of **how well the project** has done against the original Project Initiation Documentation
Enhance (risk response)	A risk **response** to an **opportunity** where proactive actions are taken to **enhance** both the probability of the event occurring and the impact of the event should it occur
Event-driven control	A control that takes place when a **specific event** occurs. This could be, for example, the **end of a stage**, the completion of the **Project Initiation Documentation**, or the creation of an **Exception Report**.
Exception	A situation where it can be **forecast** that there will be a **deviation beyond**

Practitioner Exam Tips

Introduction

This booklet aims to assist candidates who will be taking the PRINCE2 Practitioner examination.

In this booklet you will find some helpful hints on how to manage the booklets and read the information you are provided with as well as how to manage your time and some techniques you can use for answering certain styles of questions.

The Manual

The practitioner exam is an open book exam. You may bring only your OGC PRINCE2® manual with you.

You **are** allowed to tab your book to make navigation a little easier, but you **cannot** under any circumstances paste or insert any additional material into the book. You **may** however write as much additional information into the manual that you wish.

When it comes to using the manual during the exam, you will find that your time is quite tight, so there will not be much time for you to refer to the book for every question. Here are some tips to help you use your manual in the most efficient way.

- Ensure your manual is tabbed clearly so that you can navigate easily

- Too many tabs or over tabbing your manual may result in confusion

- Only use the manual when you don't know the answer but know exactly where to find it.

- DO NOT use the manual to double check answers you think you already know.

- If you have no idea of the answer to a question and no idea where to find it in the manual – don't bother looking – guess – you will only waste valuable time.

The Booklets

You will receive a sealed plastic bag in which you will find three booklets:

- **The scenario booklet** – this will be stapled and will comprise of a single page project scenario and additional information for some of the questions – there will be approximately 10 or so pages in this booklet.

- **The question booklet** – this contains the 9 questions for the project, each question could comprise of up to 3 or 4 parts (A, B and C for example) and will total 12 marks per question.

- **The answer sheets** – No – these are not the answers, but the sheets onto which you will fill in your answers.

The scenario booklet

Our first tip with this booklet is to remove just the single scenario page from this booklet, as you will quickly discover that the project scenario is relevant for every question that you answer, so having it in front of you during the exam is crucial.

Secondly, you are allowed to write and highlight on this booklet, so our next tip is to ensure that as you are reading through the project scenario, underline or highlight relevant information and write next to it in the paragraph what that information is.

If you see a statement that you think is explaining a benefit of the project, underline or highlight and annotate in the column next to it "BENEFIT". This will help tremendously when you are answering a question and remember reading something about a benefit but cannot find it quickly.

Another very important thing to note about the additional information provided in the scenario booklet is that you **DO NOT** read any of it until you have been directed to do so by a particular question. You will note that the additional information is clearly indicated to be relevant to only one particular question, so it will not be relevant at all until you reach that question. Please **DO NOT** make the mistake of reading all the additional information and thinking it is relevant for all questions as it is not.

The Question booklet

You may answer the questions in any order you like – there is no build up of a story or information – each question is completely stand alone.

However, if you do choose to start with question 5 for example, it is recommended that you complete all parts associated with Question 5 (for example Part A, Part B and Part C)
If you do not complete all parts of the question, you may find that you forget which parts you have not completed and overlook these when you are going back over the paper.

Please pay very careful attention to any words that is in **bold**. These are there for a reason – some examples may be as follows:

• **True Statements** - this means that any information provided must be considered to be true – you do not need to verify this with the scenario, just take the information as additional information as read.

• **2** – normally all questions only have one answer, except in the case of multiple response questions, in these questions, it will clearly have a number 2 in bold indicating how many selections you should make.

• **First** – Some questions ask which might be the first actions someone might take or the first product to be updated – in these cases; you need to consider only the first.

The Answer booklet

Please note: this booklet must be completed in **pencil ONLY.** It is best not to write notes or highlight in this booklet, reserve it only for your answers.

You will notice that the answer booklet clearly states which question and part of the question you are completing. It would help to be very aware of where you are completing the answers as some delegates have found themselves completing the incorrect question or part – so be alert to this.

When you begin answering your questions, it is **strongly advised** that you fill the answers directly into the answer booklet. Some delegates have tried filling the answers in on the question booklet and then transposing the answers to the answer sheets, only to make errors in transposing. You will receive **NO MARKS** for incorrect transposing as it is only the answer sheets that are marked!

At the end of the exam, **all three** booklets must be returned to the invigilator, with just the answer sheets sealed in the plastic bags provided. Your candidate number, which will be provided to you for the examination MUST appear on all three booklets in the allocated place. If you do not return any parts of the booklets, you exam may not be marked by the APM group.

Please pay very careful attentions to any words that are in **bold**. These are there for a reason – some examples may be as follows:

- **True Statements** - this means that any information provided must be considered to be true – you do not need to verify this with the scenario, just take the information as additional information as read.

- **2** – normally all questions only have one answer, except in the case of multiple response questions, in these questions, it will clearly have a number 2 in bold indicating how many selections you should make.

- **First** – Some questions ask which might be the first actions someone might take or the first product to be updated – in these cases; you need to consider only the first.

Types of questions

There are five different types of questions. These are as follows with some examples and tips on how to answer them.

1. Classic multiple choice questions
This question style is very similar to the foundation style questions with only **one** answer. The answer you select may be from 3 or 4 different options:

Example: When preparing the next stage Plan, the Project Manager identified the Project time and cost tolerances. Is this appropriate application of PRINCE2?	
A	Yes, because the Project Manager should document the time and cost tolerances for the project in the Stage Plan.
B	Yes, because the Project Manager defines the tolerances for the Project.
C	No, because Project tolerances are defined in the Project Plan.
D	No, because the Project Board define and set Project Tolerances.

Although the style of these multiple choice questions varies, the above example is one style they may give you. Once you have read the question, decide if the statement is correct or not and then you have a 50/50 chance of getting the answer correct. In the above example, the answer would be C.

2. Multiple Responses

This is the only style of question where you will select **two** answers in your answer booklet. Typically your answers would be selected from 5 options.

The best approach to this style of question is to read the question and then select the first most obvious answer. There is usually one answer which does stand out more than the others. Once you have selected your first answer, re-read the question and then look for the next most likely answer.

Example: Answer the following question about the change control procedure.	
1	**Examine:** When carrying out an impact analysis for an issue, which **2** of the following would be considered? A. The project performance targets in terms of time, cost, quality and scope. B. The Communications Management Strategy to determine who should be informed of the issue. C. The risk registers to determine if any risks are impacted by the issue. D. The exception report which raised the issue. E. The Project Business Case, especially in terms of the impact on the benefits.

Another possible approach is to read each answer and put a tick, question mark or cross next to each selection and then see what you have. You might find that you only have to select between three possible answers. Make sure when this is the case, you re-read the question in case any key words jump out which make one option more likely than another.

Example: Answer the following question about the change control procedure.	
1	**Examine:** When carrying out an impact analysis for an issue, which **2** of the following would be considered? A. The project performance targets in terms of time, cost, quality and scope. B. The Communications Management Strategy to determine who should be informed of the issue. C. The risk registers to determine if any risks are impacted by the issue. D. The exception report which raised the issue. E. The Project Business Case, especially in terms of the impact on the benefits. **The Answers are A and E**

Matching

These questions are great for catching up on time. They typically involve matching a statement in column 1 with a selection from column 2.

Please note that there is only ever **one** answer to these questions although the options in column 2 can sometimes be used only once, more than once or some not used at all.

Example: Column 1 is a list of **True Statements** about Initiating a Project. For each statement in Column 1, select from Column 2 the PRINCE2 theme being used. Each selection from Column 2 can be used once, more than once or not at all.	
Column 1	Column 2
1. The Project Manager has prepared the Project Plan. 2. Identifying which stakeholders should be communicated with during the project. 3. Setting up the risk register 4. The Project Manager identified two end stage assessments in the Project Plan.	A. Business Case B. Quality C. Risk D. Plans E. Change F. Progress G. Organization
In the above example the answer is for 1 is D, 2 is G, 3 is C and 4 is F.	

Sequencing

These questions sometimes require you to either determine just a sequence of events or sometimes even to determine is some of the statements are part of the sequence and then to sequence the remainder of the statements.

Example: Column 1 is a list of decisions to be made within the project. For each decision in Column 1, decide whether or not it is made in Starting up a Project Process and indicate in which order the decisions which are made should occur.	
Column 1	Column 2
1. Approval of the feasibility study by the Project Board before any work on the project can commence. 2. Decide if the source of funding is sufficient to fund the project's objective. 3. Assess which parties should be involved during the project, as suggested by previous development projects. 4. Evaluate two possible candidates for Project Manager and decide which should be appointed.	A. Not made in the Starting up a project process B. First C. Second D. Third E. Fourth
In the above example the answer is for 1 is A, 2 is D, 3 is C and 4 is B.	

5. Assertion/Reason

These questions are sometimes the hardest level of question and can take up a lot of your time in answering. There is however a very good technique you can use which should make it much easier to answer these questions.

The first tip we advise is for you to read each assertion statement and each reason statement as a completely standalone question. To ensure that you do this, it is strongly recommended that you read the questions on a column by column basis. All of the assertion statements will relate in some way to the scenario. All of the reason statements are generally Prince 2 statements. You will need to read each statement and determine if they are TRUE or FALSE first. As you read down each column, use a pencil to indicate T or F for each statement.

If you have any combinations with a False, your answer will either be C, D or F from the indicated table within the question.

Things get a little trickier when you have two answers which are both True. You will now need to apply an additional test to determine if the statements are A or B.

The best way to do this is to read the Reason statement first placing the word therefore in the middle and then reading the Assertion statement.

If the Reason statement explains why the Assertion statement is TRUE then the answer will be A.

If the Reason statement does not explain why the Assertion statement is true, then the answer will be B

Example: Using the Project Scenario, answer the following question.

Lines 1 to 2 in the table below consist of an assertion statement and a reason statement. For each line identify the appropriate option, from options A to E, that applies. Each option can be used once, more than once or not at all.

Option Assertion Reason
A True True AND the reason explains the assertion
B True True BUT the reason does not explain the assertion
C True False
D False True
E False False

Assertion		Reason	
1	The expected benefits from increasing staff flexibility should be included in the business case.	BECAUSE	All known business case benefits should be described clearly in measurable terms.
2	The expected benefits from increasing staff flexibility should be included in the business case.	BECAUSE	Information about expected project benefits forms part of the justification for undertaking a project.

In the above example both assertion and reason statements are true, but in line 1, the reason statement is stating that all benefits should be described in measurable terms, but the assertion statement does not describe a measurable benefit, it only states that expected benefits should be included. For this reason, the answer for the first line is B.

In the second line, the reason statement is explaining that expected benefits help to justify the project starting and continuing which does in fact explain why expected benefits should be included in the business case so therefore the answer to the second line is A.

Other tips for answering questions:

Another type of question that is often asked in the exam is where a sample management product is provided for example a Quality Management Strategy, and you are provided with a draft which contains errors. When you get this type of question, do not attempt to read all the additional information as it will not necessarily all make sense.

A good technique you can use is as follows:

• Start by finding the correct management product in Appendix A to use as reference while answering the question

• Next read only the first question, but do not look at the answers yet

• Then read each entry in the section you are directed to look at and decide whether you feel that statement is correct and fits there. If you don't think it is appropriate, circle the item or put a mark against it

• When you have finished reading each of the entries under that heading, look at the proposed answers – you should be able to match up the items you found to be incorrect with the answers pretty easily.

This technique will be demonstrated by your trainer, but it generally works most of the time.

Timings

As most of you will probably gather, time is going to be your enemy during the exam. You cannot afford a leisurely pace as the suggested timings are as follows:

- 10 Minutes to read the scenario
- 15 Minutes for each of the 9 questions
- 10 Minutes tolerance for additional reading

These are really tight and most delegates finish with little time to spare. It is strongly recommended that you fill in your answer book as you go along and try to keep up a steady methodical pace.

Best of Luck

Printed in Great Britain
by Amazon.co.uk, Ltd.,
Marston Gate.